The Busy Doctor's
INVESTMENT GUIDE

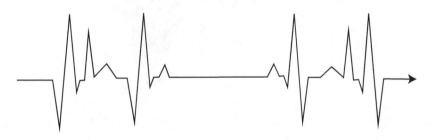

The Busy Doctor's
INVESTMENT GUIDE

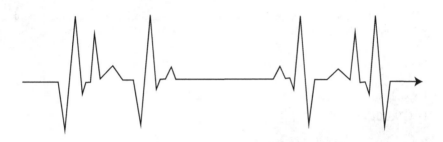

How

ONE ADJUSTMENT PER MONTH
Can Save and Maintain Your Portfolio's Health

David Yeh, M.D.

Published by Advantage, Charleston, South Carolina.
Member of Advantage Media Group.

ADVANTAGE is a registered trademark and the Advantage colophon is a trademark of Advantage Media Group, Inc.

Printed in the United States of America.

ISBN: 978-1-59932-552-1
LCCN: 2015937803

This publication is designed to provide accurate and authoritative information in regard to the subject matter covered. It is sold with the understanding that the publisher is not engaged in rendering legal, accounting, or other professional services. If legal advice or other expert assistance is required, the services of a competent professional person should be sought.

Advantage Media Group is proud to be a part of the Tree Neutral® program. Tree Neutral offsets the number of trees consumed in the production and printing of this book by taking proactive steps such as planting trees in direct proportion to the number of trees used to print books. To learn more about Tree Neutral, please visit **www.treeneutral.com**. To learn more about Advantage's commitment to being a responsible steward of the environment, please visit **www.advantagefamily.com/green**

Advantage Media Group is a publisher of business, self-improvement, and professional development books and online learning. We help entrepreneurs, business leaders, and professionals share their Stories, Passion, and Knowledge to help others Learn & Grow. Do you have a manuscript or book idea that you would like us to consider for publishing? Please visit **advantagefamily.com** or call **1.866.775.1696**.

ACKNOWLEDGMENTS

I would like to thank my wife, Liwei, for her patience as I wrote this book. To my son, William: Thank you for being the inspiration for this book, the reason to leave a legacy. For the next generation of physicians, my desire is to continue to provide a message of hope despite these increasingly uncertain times. And finally, my thanks to Tony Robbins and my fellow graduates of his courses who have since become an incredible peer group and family to me. You were the incredible source of inspiration and support that sparked the genesis of this book. Keep sparking.

CONTENTS

Introduction 11

CHAPTER 1: How I Got Started 17

CHAPTER 2: My Philosophy of Investing 25

CHAPTER 3: Dollar Cost Averaging—A Good Start 39

CHAPTER 4: The 20-Month Moving Average: Adding an Exit Strategy ... 53

CHAPTER 5: The Monthly Rotation Investment System: Background 63

CHAPTER 6: Putting the MRI to Work 75

CHAPTER 7: Dealing with Stock Tips 87

CHAPTER 8: The Psychology of Investing 103

CHAPTER 9: Common Questions and Answers 119

CHAPTER 10: Conclusion 131

INTRODUCTION

Here's a party trick for you: Take a $20 bill out of your pocket and ask someone to rip it in half. That's right. Have someone tear that $20 bill right down the middle into two pieces. Most people can't do it. We all know the bill is just a piece of paper, but still, our stomachs feel queasy at the thought of tearing it up. People can say money isn't that important to them, but rip a piece of paper with Andrew Jackson's face on it and, believe me, the pain is palpable.

To deny the role that money plays in our lives is a big mistake. Sure, there are lots of things in life that are important: family, friends, work, health, and community. But money is equally important, even if we pretend it's not. High schools teach economics but don't teach students how to finance a college education. Family conversations about budgets and finances are whispered. If there is any emphasis on money at all, it tends to be on how to make it, not what to do with it after we make it. The widespread stereotype of wealthy physicians is antithetical, whereas the stereotype of physicians being, for the most part, notoriously poor investors, is deadly accurate.

As physicians, we are trained in the science and art of medicine. We are not trained in business. We are not trained in finances, nor are we trained in negotiation skills. We understand pathology: how to recognize it and how to treat it. This is not to say we aren't smart enough to grasp the concepts of business and finances. We are. It's not easy to become a doctor. It takes a lot of education, training, hours, and sacrifice. But when we finally get our medical degrees, we find ourselves ill prepared to make money, even with a successful practice, let alone keep and grow money. Running any business is difficult enough without the unique pressures of running a medical practice.

My father is a doctor. And for my father's generation of physicians, it was enough to just make money with a successful practice. But the landscape for doctors has changed. A private practice is not something you can fully rely on, because of the expense involved in running it and the uncertainty of the direction medicine is taking. A private practice doesn't net as much as it used to due to increasing overhead costs and regulations, declining reimbursements from third-party payers, and malpractice insurance. Medical education, from medical school (with its student loan burdens and progressively worsening loan terms) and required continued medical education, hobbles us financially from the get-go. Increasing liability and regulatory costs such as those inherent in the Health Insurance Privacy and Portability Act (HIPPA), mandatory electronic medical records (EMR), and the Patient Protection and Affordable Care Act continue to shrink revenues and increase expenses. Malpractice premiums continue to rise. Statistics show that doctors have a 75–99 percent lifetime risk of facing a malpractice claim, depending on specialty.[1] We're sued not because we are incompetent but because of bad outcomes, which are almost inevitable in any busy practice. Even world-famous authorities have been sued. And with skyrocketing jackpot judgments, sometimes malpractice insurance isn't enough. This is why it is up to you to mind your own finances and transform what modest income you have left into wealth while you still can.

---

1 Anupam B., et al, N Engl J Med 2011; 365:629-636

Ultimately, it is not about how you make money but what you do with it, and what you do with it need not be complicated. In fact, it can take as little as a few minutes per month, but it must be regular, and it must be disciplined. Some physicians say, "I have a broker. I just let them do it." First, let me ask you if you know the difference between abdication and delegation. Outsourcing something as important as your financial future without remaining engaged is a sure recipe for disaster. Second, if you decide to remain engaged in your financial future, do you understand what your broker does? Third, and most important, do you know your broker's risk management strategy? It is vital to understand your investments and why you are in them. You wouldn't go into a business without understanding the risks of the business. You wouldn't make a bet without understanding the risks of the bet. As physicians, we always weigh risks against benefits before prescribing tests or treatment plans for patients. It should be the same with investments. You shouldn't invest in a stock or other security unless you at least understand the basic risks. Even if you have a broker who is an adequate stock picker or asset allocator, what happens when another bear market comes along, like the one in 2000 or the one in 2007? What's your broker's risk management strategy, other than positioning your investments in a pie chart and rebalancing? Kudos if your broker or money manager can explain all that in a way you can understand and trust, but red flags if your broker or money manager likes to use words such as *think* and *feel*—for example, "We will reallocate into X if we *feel* the market will…"

We are trained as physicians to identify a problem, work it up, and prescribe a solution. Similarly, when we buy a stock, we tend to identify an acute problem and prescribe a final solution by buying the stock. Done. A better analogy would be that buying the asset is just the beginning, not the final solution, of the process of managing a chronic condition. The ultimate outcome of the process is when you eventually get out of the market. The solution is the exit strategy.

Last year, at the age of 45, I was able to semi-retire. When I tell my colleagues this, their number-one question is how I can semi-retire at such a young age. My answer is in this book. It's a system for investing that I developed and call the MRI, which stands for Monthly Rotation Investment system. When I explain the MRI system to colleagues, they often ask if I will manage their money too. My answer to that question was to develop the Wealthy Doctor Institute. Through the Wealthy Doctor Institute I try to help other doctors create another revenue source, developing a critical capital mass with a revenue stream that can take care of at least basic living expenses. Imagine working because you want to work, without the financial pressures of having to work. Sure, you could outsource the management of your assets. But I want to teach you how to manage your own assets because, quite frankly, no one will watch your nest egg more closely than you will. Most physicians like us focus on making money to take care of our future. However, few realize it's what you do with your money, not how much you make, that is key to sustained wealth. The problem with only focusing on making money is that you are trading your time, the most precious commodity you have, for money. But when you focus on what you *do* with the money you make, you are leveraging your knowledge and skills to grow another income stream, basically creating another business with no employees and no lawsuits.

In my radiology practice, I've always looked for ways to make improvements. I look for better ways of scanning, better ways of improving my protocols. When I was on the Tai Chi tournament circuit, I always practiced with the aim of improving. Even when commuting, I challenge myself to find a better, faster, or more interesting route. So when I began investing, I asked myself the same kinds of questions: How can I be more successful? How can I more precisely define "success"? (Clarity of outcome vastly improves chances of success.) What other weaknesses am I not seeing, and how can I overcome weaknesses in my strategy? How can I better protect my money while still making reasonable investment gains? It's that mentality of always trying to improve that drove me, as a young intern, to go from being naïve about money to being semi-retired less than 20 years later. The fact that you are reading this book indicates you share this value of continuous, never-ending improvement, and I congratulate you.

TAKEAWAYS:

Investing success requires more than a magic mechanical formula. Mechanical formulas are commonplace. Our minds and our emotions, ultimately, need to be aligned with our goals. The emotional, gut-wrenching difficulty of ripping in half a simple $20 bill demonstrates how seriously we need to deal with our emotions before we can effectively handle any mechanical formulas.

1
CHAPTER

HOW I GOT STARTED

I wasn't born with a silver spoon in my mouth. My parents grew up in occupied Taiwan during the war. They lived in poverty, with three generations crammed together in one house. Partly through luck and partly because he was smart and worked hard, my dad was able to pass the exam that allowed him to go to medical school. Upon completing his studies in Taiwan, he moved to Canada to do his training. At that time, anti-Chinese immigration laws made it difficult to move directly to the United States. The closest he could get was Canada, where my parents resided in a basement, eating chicken necks for dinner because those were the cheapest meats they could buy from the butcher.

I was born in Canada, but once my parents became Canadian citizens and were able to move us to the United States, they did so.

I was five years old. It was then that the new technology of computerized tomography (CT) and ultrasound was emerging. My dad became one of the pioneers of ultrasound. He practiced in New York City while I grew up in suburban New Jersey. But despite his success, the takeaway messages about money in our household were 1) save like crazy, 2) don't flaunt your wealth, and 3) be humble and don't take any chances. That frugal mentality served my dad well. As a result, I was able to attend Cornell and then New York University Medical School without accruing any debt.

But in other ways, his frugal mentality did not serve me well. I was a physician, an intern straight out of medical school, with my first paycheck in hand, and I didn't have the first idea of how to manage money. My parents had financially insulated me for my entire life. Somehow, despite my "frugality," I racked up a lot of credit card debt. I had reached a point of success and yet felt like a failure because I couldn't get a handle on the financial part of my life. The truth was that not only was I ignorant about money but I also labored under a lot of misconceptions about money. I grew up watching television shows and movies that taught me rich people were evil, money corrupted, and greed was immoral.

I had always wanted to be a good, giving person. It's one of the reasons I became a doctor. I believe it's what drives a lot of us physicians. We sacrifice years of our lives in education and training. We are not driven to do so just to make money. There are far easier paths to wealth than becoming a physician. I had seen my dad sacrifice and struggle to become the physician he was. He had never been driven to do so by money. In fact, he lived a pretty aesthetic life and passed on those values.

So there I stood as an intern, broke and in debt. And being frugal was all I had learned from my dad about money. But frugality carries with it a scarcity mentality. And in the same way that patients who constantly think of themselves as sick tend to get sick all the time, if we set our minds to the belief that money is scarce in our lives, money will be scarce. That frugal mindset did not help me at all in the real world of the 1990s.

I finally reached a point of desperation at which I decided to get control of my finances. I learned to take a new attitude to money, starting with the idea that it's not a necessary evil; it's just *necessary*. Money makes a good person more capable of good and an evil person more capable of evil. It may be true that money can't buy love, but money is still as necessary as oxygen to make living possible. And an honest accounting of our finances is a very concrete way to measure our honesty and integrity. I started reading self-help books and discovered some simple, yet common, concepts, such as paying yourself first, dollar cost averaging, and compound interest. Despite the fact that these ideas had been around for years, they were all new ideas to me. I read that just by saving $2,000 a year, it is possible to retire with a million dollars (see figure1.1 on the next page). To a broke young intern, this was amazing news! It gave me hope.

I was so excited by these concepts that I began doing my own calculations using Excel spreadsheets. I had to prove to myself that these ideas could work. Granted, the 12 percent a year in figure 1.1 is an optimistic number, but to be fair, neither is it unrealistic. However, the underlying concepts of forced savings, dollar cost averaging, and compound interest served as a great starting point for me.

TWINS ANNE AND BETH'S SAVINGS EXAMPLE

AGE	ANNE	BETH
22	$2,000.00	
23	$2,000.00	
24	$2,000.00	
25	$2,000.00	
26	$2,000.00	
27	$2,000.00	
28		$2,000.00
29		$2,000.00
30		$2,000.00
59		$2,000.00
60		$2,000.00
61		$2,000.00
62		$2,000.00
63		$2,000.00
64		$2,000.00
65		$2,000.00
Ending Balance:	$1.2 Million ($1,203,963.99)	$1.2 Million ($1,219,661.07)

Figure 1.1. At 22 years of age, Anne saves $2,000 per year for six years and then never saves another cent in her life. Her twin sister Beth, however, goes to college and otherwise explores life for six years without saving a cent but then systematically saves $2,000 per year starting at age 28 until she retires at age 65. They both invest in a mutual fund that returns 12 percent/year. At the age of 65, Beth remarks to Anne, "Wow, I've been disciplined. I've been saving every year without fail for the last 37 years, and now I have $1.2 million in my account," to which Anne says, "Isn't that interesting? That's how much I have too." Moral: start saving and investing as soon as you can. Don't delay.

So step one was to face the fact that I was ignorant about money and that my mind, ego, and emotions were closing me off from seeking education. Step two was to begin to educate myself. And step three was to take action. I went to my bank and talked to a broker about dollar cost averaging in a mutual fund, at $50 per month, and then I went to the human resources department at work and set up an automatic funding system for my retirement account. It doesn't seem like a lot now, but back then, I was broke, and at the end of the month, there was more month than there was money. So this was a huge sacrifice for me. The important thing is that I was making a mental shift to be on the correct side of the growth curve instead of the wrong side of the debt curve. And I kept studying finance and investing strategies because I wanted to tweak that growth curve, tweak my forced savings, and see if I could improve the outcome.

After a couple of years, I had accumulated about $5,000—not a fortune, true, but a decent amount that was accrued during a bull market, despite high fees. The good news was that I learned how to open an investment account. The forms and regulations didn't intimidate me. So I opened a no-load fund (low-fee) account on my own. I would later learn that published fees were not the only costs that took their toll on returns. I came across a video course on investing through stock options, which promised fantastic returns, so I took it. It cost me $2,000, which was a big sum for me at that time. But I devoured the information and tracked the web page that accompanied the course so I could follow along how the instructor's trades were doing. As I followed the live trades online, I could see that the trades made by the video course instructor weren't actually doing that well. I could see why they weren't doing well when I tried to second-guess how I would have traded, based on the information available to me at that time. Being able to see the problem allowed me to play with it and fine-tune it and figure out what I could do differently to improve the outcome. And that's how I learned. It's also how the worst thing that could happen to a beginning investor happened to me.

The worst thing that can happen to a first-time investor is not to lose money but to be wildly successful. By the second trade, I had made a profit of more than 100 percent. I thought I was a genius, until I crashed my $5,000 account with my very next trade. But rather than be discouraged, I knew that consistent success was possible.

So I kept learning. I learned new concepts, such as position sizing and risk management. And I kept trading. And I continued to be successful. I was so successful that my protective puts (options) and stop losses shielded me from much of the market bloodbath that was the dot-com bubble burst of 2000–2002. By then, I felt I was a bulletproof genius again, only more so. For the next 17 months, I made 17 consecutive successful trades and thought I was so untouchable I could ignore some of my own trading rules and still be successful. And then, on the eighteenth trade, I lost—almost everything.

During the 1990s, when everything was pretty much still going up, I learned that even in a bull market, it was still possible to lose. The good news is I learned that lesson early in my investing life. I learned that risk management is an important component in investing. And because I had learned this lesson hard and well early on, I was able to survive the crash of 2000–2002, as well as the crash of 2007–2008, using more refined yet simpler strategies.

I had just finished my fellowship and was starting my private practice when the bear market of 2000–2002 hit. I already had a whole bunch of money in high-tech stocks. But when the stock market started crashing, all of my stop losses were triggered. Normally, one or two stop losses might get triggered every few months or so, but in one month that year, almost every one of my stop losses triggered. Something *big* was happening in the stock market. Conversely, my colleagues were all in a buying frenzy, picking up high-tech stocks, thinking they were getting a bargain. Others kept holding on to falling stocks because they didn't have an investment or exit strategy. And me? I was out of the market with my risk money. And I did not have an entry strategy at that point because none of the stocks were meeting my purchasing criteria.

So I was protected, but it was painful to watch my colleagues who were dying slow, financial deaths at the time. The sad thing was they were truly confident they were doing the right thing by staying in the market. After a few months, I told them, "Look, I'm out. How much pain does it take for you to realize that it's time to get out?" A couple of other physicians listened and got out, but most stayed in till the end. And by 2002 their 401(k)s had become 201(k)s. I knew a physician who was in his late fifties and ready to retire and who ended up working 14 more years to make up for his losses. He was only able to retire just recently.

Nineteen years ago I knew very little about money, finances, or investing. I taught myself, made mistakes, learned from them, and developed and refined systems that allowed me to semi-retire in less than two decades. As I write this, I am 45 years old and married, with a ten-year-old son. Instead of being part of a busy private practice where I am on call nights and weekends, I work at an imaging center where the workload is relatively light. I have no nights and no weekends. I have time to spend time with my son, who is growing up quickly. I have the freedom to attend his extracurricular activities. I'm there for his teacher conferences, school performances, and tournaments. To be in control of your own time becomes increasingly important because time is more precious as you age. It is the one commodity you can't use your money to buy. Once, when I was younger, I attended an investment seminar. A question was asked of the older investors: if they had just one piece of advice to give to younger investors, what would it be? A cacophony of "Invest now! Don't wait!" erupted. This has stuck with me: Invest now. Don't wait.

TAKEAWAYS:

Money management and investing can be learned. Mastery of the emotions underlying money and wealth is more important than learning the mechanical skills of investing. Losses can happen even in a bull market; learning to minimize losses can save you in a bear market. Time is on your side if you start now; the future is closer than you realize.

CHAPTER

MY PHILOSOPHY OF INVESTING

WHY OUR PSYCHOLOGY AND EMOTIONS SABOTAGE OUR INVESTMENTS, AND WHY WE NEED SYSTEMS

The one thing I hear most often regarding investing is "I wish I had started 20 years ago." These are the same people who say, "I can always do this later." Because our future self is so abstract, we don't pay much attention to it. Instead, we focus on the urgent: our present selves, our present family, and our present work situation. But it is what we focus on in life that grows. I am not advocating focusing exclusively on investing and improving ourselves as investors. There are other areas of life we need to balance in our lives as well, such as work, family, and health. To completely neglect the financial part of our lives, however, is foolhardy.

In figure 1.1, I showed you the example of twins Anne and Beth, who each amassed $1.2 million just by investing regularly. Anne contributed only $12,000 total, whereas Beth contributed $74,000. How can this be? Simple. Anne started six years earlier. Time was on her side, and time is very powerful. Reading that story woke me up. I opened that investment account with the bank, put in $50 a month for two years, and continued learning more about investing, particularly about no-load funds.

During the next two years, I learned about no-load funds that might have outperformed my funds, which, at that time, were managed by a brokerage. I opened up my trusty Excel spreadsheet again and compared historical data corrected for dividends. I closed my high-load account and invested in my first no-load fund. When I learned how to trade options, I opened an options-enabled brokerage account and started trading options. I was wildly successful at first, but then, I devastated my account. That experience taught me three important lessons: 1) the shattering power of losses, 2) the importance of exit strategies, and 3) the need to understand the risks involved in whatever I was investing in.

Let's take those lessons one at a time. People often don't fully appreciate how losses can affect your account. If you lose 10 percent of your portfolio, it will take an 11 percent gain just to break even. If you lose 25 percent, it will take 33 percent to break even. And if you lose 50 percent, it will take 100 percent to break even. Losses are bigger than you think. And if you were to suffer a 90 percent loss, you would have to make 900 percent back to break even (see figure 2.1).

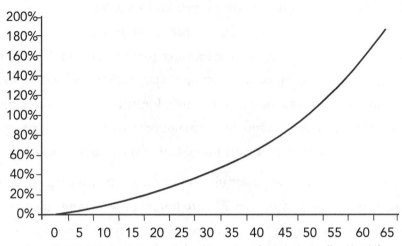

% Gain Needed to Break Even

Figure 2.1. How much do you need to gain (y-axis) to make up for the loss you suffered (x-axis)?

In my case, while the numbers weren't big, the percentages were significant. I plummeted from $5,000 to just about $1,000 in my account. But my first thought wasn't, "Gee, I should have stuck with a broker." Instead, it was lesson number two: "I should have had a better exit strategy." Five different investors investing at the same time in the same stock can all end up differently, from successful to devastated, all due to one thing: differences in their exit strategies. I had been successful in the past, so I knew success was possible. I saw winning trades turn into losses because I was too greedy to pull the trigger and get out or too fearful of losing out on future gains. I also saw trades go against me, and I was too fearful and worshiped my ego too much to "lock in a loss," to get out at a smaller loss. Thus, I really had no one to blame but myself. I had to examine why I had lost the money, which meant looking at my trade to see when there might have been a better time to get out of the market. I had to recognize exit opportunities as they occurred and refine my exit strategies. Blaming the banker, the market, the news, the price of oil, or terrorists for my loss would have been the same as saying I had no control over my own money. So I took what I had left and implemented lesson number three: risk management. I started with smaller trades, spent more time learning about what I was investing in, got a better grasp of the risks and characteristics of what I was trading, and became more conservative. I learned these lessons early enough to mitigate and survive the major bear markets of the twenty-first century while others were losing half of their portfolios—twice.

You can see how powerfully emotions affect investing. And if you guessed that having rules is key to improving investing outcomes, you would be correct. For instance, take the typical investor, who trades without trading rules: no entry rule, no exit rule, just sees a graph of, say, the S&P 500 index in 1996 (see figure 2.2).

Figure 2.2. "Stocks have gone up so much already it's too dangerous to buy!"

In 1996 the massive bull run had barely begun. Dot-coms were barely in the news. The concept of a "Goldilocks economy" (not too hot, not too cold) wasn't in the news yet, and the typical investor thought stocks had already gone too high too fast and thus were too dangerous an investment. That line of thinking would not have served the investor well, because come year 2000 (see figure 2.3):

THE S&P 500 INDEX 1993–2000
(USING VFINX AS PROXY)

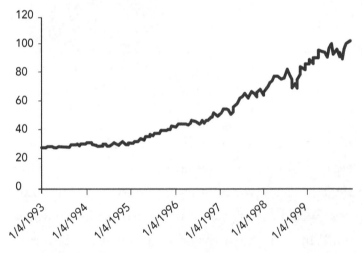

Figure 2.3. "Stocks just keep going up. I've missed out on so much already. Where's the 'buy' button?"

Of course, stocks had risen 130 percent between 1996 and 2000. The media was gushing about the "this-time-it's-different" Goldilocks economy and dot-coms. This attitude did not serve investors well either, as the very next year, the S&P 500 looked like this (see figure 2.4).

THE S&P 500 INDEX 1997–2001
(USING VFINX AS PROXY)

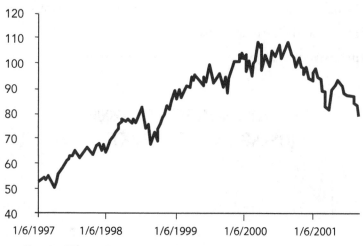

Figure 2.4. "Aaargh! It's only a dip, right? Right?"

For seemingly no reason, there was a 53 percent wipeout from the peak of 2000. Accounting irregularities that were celebrated in the 1990s were now vilified as scapegoats for stock crashes and bankruptcies. Would trading rules have helped the investor make better decisions? In the next few chapters, I will illustrate how even one or two simple rules can improve trading outcomes.

After the first bear market of the early 2000s I was back making money again. It was a bull market, and I was using fairly complex options strategies. I had survived the bear market, and I was consistently making monthly income in this bull market. I thought I was king of the world. I was using a complex options strategy, but it had rules. I became successful for so long that I got cocky and broke six out of seven of my own rules. Again, I wound up shattered. There I was with a six-figure account, more money than I had ever had in my life, and I had lost almost all of it. I was down to five digits. But that wasn't the worst of it. I had lost almost all of my parents' money, too. I had been doing so well with my own money that my dad had entrusted me with his money, and now it was gone. I couldn't sleep at night. I had knots in my stomach bigger than when I was a broke intern only nine years before. Sure, I hated losing my own money, but I was young and could recover. Losing someone else's money, on the other hand, in particular my parents', was far worse. In fact, it was the worst feeling in the world.

Is it possible to fail even with trading rules? Yes, trading rules are not perfect, but more importantly, *not* following trading rules is a surefire way to fail. Trading rules, if properly structured and faithfully followed, can decrease the chances of large losses over the long term. But I cannot overemphasize the power of emotions to override faith in even the simplest set of rules.

I want to take a moment here to emphasize why you need a system if you want to invest. Often, people approach investing in the same way they approach relationships and sex: "If it ain't spontaneous, it ain't worth doing." The opposite is actually true; methods matter in everything in life. The old, fat, bald, pickup artist who has calibrated his social radar and refined his "dating" approach to a science of a well-executed system will trump your spontaneous pick-up line almost every time. I'm not condoning pickup artists, only illustrating that almost any skill can be systematized. Methods matter; methods have rules. Those who have developed a system to do something bigger, better, and faster than you will trounce you in business, love, and war. The good news is that systems need not be developed from scratch. You bought this book to open your mind to the possibilities offered by investing systems. You bought this book to learn investing methods and systems that follow a set of rules.

As an investor, you are your own worst enemy. It is no coincidence that the market tends to tank when you buy and bounce back when you sell. The fact is there are millions of others out there who think much like you do and do the same things you do at approximately the same time you do them. Any mechanical system that can help you overrule your emotionally driven desire to take certain actions, or your emotionally driven timing in taking certain actions, will be beneficial because the system works outside the realm of collective greed and fear. Warren Buffet is rightly famous for saying, "Be greedy when others are fearful, and be fearful when others are greedy." Acting against your instincts is extremely hard.

The good news is it is possible to build systems that overcome or even exploit the fallibility of the collective greed and fear that characterizes the stock market. Successful systems are a dime a dozen and range from simple systems with few rules to complex systems requiring hundreds of analysts, supercomputers, complex software, and even specialized infrastructure/hardware. If you read that sentence correctly, you'll realize successful systems need not be complex. This book will describe four of them.

Systems are worthless, however, if they're not followed. In the past, I have taught and coached colleagues on simple systems. They were intelligent colleagues who routinely analyzed pages and pages of Excel spreadsheet data in doing their research for medical journals. I've sat down next to them to go over the rules and what we saw in the market and how that related to the rules. I would ask them the critical question: "So what do the rules tell you to do now?" In cases where the correct answer would have been "Sell," I would hear, instead, an ecstatic "Buy more!"

It made me want to bang my head against the wall or pull my hair out. I could not, ethically, grab my colleagues by the lapels and force them to follow the rules. They honestly thought they were "doing the right thing," even though the rules and data right in front of them told them something else. I watched these slow shipwrecks of otherwise-intelligent colleagues steer their rudders right into icebergs. This is how the power of emotion overrides even the simplest and most concrete of systems.

Consider this: as physicians, when we order tests, we are obligated to follow up on those tests. We only order the minimum number of tests to fine-tune our differential and formulate a plan going forward. If we overtest a patient, we end up with spurious, distracting data that ultimately causes more harm than good. Our investment account is our patient. Every time we read the news, we are in fact performing a test, extracting information to help narrow our differential of whether the market is likely to go up, down, or sideways. If we neglect to test "our patient" for too long, we won't know whether the market is likely to crash until it is too late.

Consider also that CEOs can lie—not because they're bad people but because their duties to their companies conflict with their duties to the stockholders. Remember CEOs work for their company; they do not work for you. Financial statements can lie. Key indicators of performance can be so deeply buried or obfuscated that even seasoned analysts can miss them. Analysts are inherently unreliable. If all the analysts were to say, "The market will go up," then, most likely, everyone would have already bought in, resulting in the probability that the market would go down instead. If all the analysts were to say, "The market is terrible," that would probably be the best time to buy. Pundits can also lie. They hold forth on their television soapboxes, not to improve your portfolio but to sell their shows. The more they exaggerate the financial news, the darker the picture they paint, and the more addictive the emotions they can trigger in their audience, the more likely their audience is to tune in again the next day.

So what can you trust? The only tools I have found reliable are price charts. Price charts document every footprint made by every trade that occurred. Remember trades are made when a seller who thinks the stock is going down sells to a buyer who thinks the stock is going up. The seller and buyer think each other mistaken, but only one will be proven correct, either in the short term or the long term.

All these data are freely available and up to date on the Internet. Do your own homework on what you want to invest in. Understand the system you're using to invest. Then, once you implement the system, stick with it. Don't half follow the system. That's a certain recipe for disaster. Don't mix or modify systems on the fly, particularly if your money is already invested. Remember, changing your plan while you're still invested means you have no plan at all.

Another factor that will play with your emotions is the herd mentality. When everyone buys the stock and there's almost no one left to buy is when the stock peaks and starts to go down. Joe Kennedy is famously quoted for selling right before the Great Crash of 1929 because even the shoeshine boy was talking about buying stocks. People will worry that they're losing their money, but no one will sell, even as the stock continues to go down. Why? Because they keep hoping the stock will go up again until it finally goes down so much that even the least savvy investor sells. Everyone is out by then, and *that's* when the stock will start to go up again. Not believing that it will really go up again, people won't jump back in again right away. This is why we have systems. Systems can help detect these trends without second-guessing. The strategies I work with focus on simple mathematical systems that require discipline once per month. More complicated systems exist that work just as well, but they require more discipline to execute.

Patient rounding is similar to using a mechanical investing system in that a patient's history is full of red herrings; only a few bits of information are actually key. Tests help to identify key, perhaps pathognomonic, data. All the other data are ancillary and irrelevant. Mechanical systems also utilize only a few, relevant bits of data to signal that a portfolio adjustment is necessary. Let the system tell you when to get in and when to get out, not your gut or your just-as-clueless brother-in-law or some television pundit.

We all have so much going on in life that we feel we can't make time for one more thing, such as investing. And indeed, there are some things in life that are urgent and other things in life that are important. It's often the important but not urgent things that make the most difference. For instance, making time to exercise, carving out time to spend with our families and loved ones, ensuring that we get an adequate amount of sleep, and making time to invest all impact importantly on our lives in the long run. And our ultimate destiny lies in the long run. People who believe money isn't as important as health and relationships should picture themselves 20 years from now when they will wish they had started investing today.

By dealing with money now, you are taking care of your future. People often don't look at the future in this way. They might have financial planners to help them plan their estates, but aside from that, they don't really look at the future very closely. They think it's so far away they can procrastinate on investing and saving, or maybe, they tell themselves they will start to save after reaching some other short-term financial goal. The problem with short-term financial goals is that they seem to multiply and fill our lives if we do not contain them. In the same way that gas fills the volume in the container that contains it, or that work fills the time contained by a deadline, short-term financial goals expand to absorb all our income. If we say we never have time to check our money and manage it, or that we don't have any money to save, we are just making excuses. We are telling ourselves a story that over time we come to believe. That's the danger.

Consider Mike Tyson, who earned close to half a *billion* dollars with a "B" during his prime as a professional boxer. Rather than retiring comfortably, "Iron Mike" is now in such an unstable position financially that he has to resort to making movies, such as "The Hangover," and other odd jobs just to maintain his lifestyle. He's effectively bankrupt. Michael Jackson, who reportedly signed a recording contract worth almost $1 billion, was forced to the brink of bankruptcy in 2007 when he was unable to pay back a $25 million loan. Kim Basinger, highly sought after and highly paid actress— bankrupt. Elton John, internationally famous and highly paid entertainer—bankrupt. Then, consider Theodore Johnson, whose first job was with the newly formed United Parcel Service in 1924. He never made more than $14,000 a year. However, by saving 20 percent of his paycheck and investing, he amassed $70 million by the time he was 90 years old.

It's not what you make but what you do with what you make that determines if you live the rest of your life in comfort or from paycheck to paycheck. The long-term success of a system points to the high probability that it will continue to work successfully in the future. Nothing works 100 percent, but even a 51 percent success rate beats a 49 percent success rate. One is profitable; one is not.

Those who invest without a system can, if they're honest, attest to the fact that success is often more the exception than the rule.

If you have a plan as you enter the market but then change the plan before you exit, you really have no plan at all. To be successful, your plan needs risk management and exit strategies. What often happens, though, is that you will have a plan going in, and then, something distracts you from it, perhaps the financial news, a statement from your company's CEO, or your brother-in-law's so-called blinding flash of insight. So you deviate from your plan, and in doing so, you increase your chances of losing money. Victory is not about making money; victory is about successfully following the rules that you have set up before committing your first dollar to any one trade and that you do not violate until you exit the trade. In the coming chapters, we'll look at some systems, including the MRI I developed, and I will show you how you can follow them successfully.

TAKEAWAYS:

A good investing system is important for all the reasons we've discussed: taking responsibility, avoiding losses, starting early, and dealing with our emotions. But even though systems are a dime a dozen, a system can only work to the extent that you follow it with discipline.

DOLLAR COST AVERAGING— A GOOD START

Let's begin by looking at a prototypical concept or "system" every beginner investor needs to understand: dollar cost averaging. The principle is that you invest a fixed amount of money into the market at fixed periodic intervals. For example, if you had $100,000 to invest, you might split up the hundred grand into $5,000 increments and invest that amount each year for the next 20 years. In other words, you put the same amount into the market each period, forever. Now, I've actually heard people say, "Oh, I'm just going to dollar cost average my $100,000 into the market, $10,000 at a time, per month." That's not dollar cost averaging, because after ten months, you are completely invested, and you don't put any more money in.

Money managers love dollar cost averaging because it's a form of forced savings, forcing you to pay yourself first before paying any other mandatory or voluntary expense. And the logic of forced savings is indisputable: every book on wealth creation, personal finance, and money management agrees that spending less than you make is key. People with paychecks get their money on a periodic basis, and with dollar cost averaging, they automatically pay themselves on a periodic basis. So for instance, those who put $5,000 a year into their IRA are making a periodic investment every year. The problem here is that the law frequently changes the amount that can be invested per year, so investors can't follow true dollar cost averaging. Technically, the same can be said about corporate 401(k) accounts or other retirement plans. But whether we call it forced savings or dollar cost averaging, the concept is the same: a fixed amount is invested periodically. It doesn't matter what periods you set up as long as you are consistent with them. It is a simple system with that one rule.

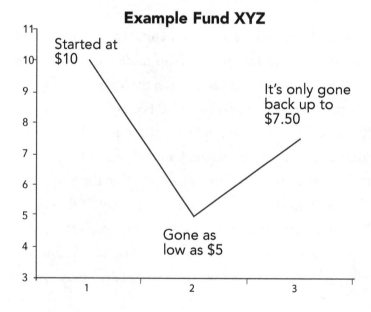

Figure 3.1.

Let's look at an example. Figure 3.1 shows a hypothetical mutual fund, XYZ. In year one, the fund is priced at $10 per share. In year two, the fund is priced at $5 per share. And in year three, it's priced at $7.50 per share. Normally, anyone looking at this graph would tell us we're not doing very well. We've lost half of our money. We haven't even broken even yet! It's a terrible investment. Or it's a terrible time to be investing. But with dollar cost averaging, we would put in the same amount of money each time. So in year one, at $10 a share, had we put in $1,000, we would have bought 100 shares. In year two, when we bought in at $5 a share, we put $1,000 in and would have bought 200 shares. And in year three, at $7.50 a share, we would have bought 133.333 shares. So the total we have in is $1,000 plus $1,000 plus $1,000 over three years, which equals $3,000. Our total shares bought are 100 plus 200 plus 133.333, which totals 433.333 shares. Multiply that by the $7.50 share price, which is where the shares are at year three, and we have $3,250.00 in our portfolio. So even though the price of the mutual fund has been trending down, because we put in the same amount each time, when the prices were lower, we were forced to buy more shares at the lower price, and thus we came out ahead.

It may feel counterintuitive because we instinctively calculate our average share price to be $7.50 if we bought shares at $10, $5, and $7.50. However, the average share price is $6.92 (see figure 3.2). Our average price is the harmonic mean of our historical prices. In dollar cost averaging, when the share price goes up, we automatically buy fewer shares, but we're happy that the market is going up. And when the share price goes down, we're happy that we're automatically buying more shares. That's right. With dollar cost averaging, we're happy whether the market goes up or down!

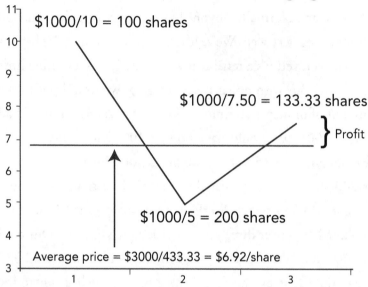

Figure 3.2.

Now let's use the same fund but change the order of the prices. This time Fund XYZ goes from $5 a share to $7.50 a share to $10 a share. We are still putting $1,000 in per year, and we have the same average price. Thus, we have bought the same number of shares: 433.333 shares. But now the price per share at year three is $10, so we actually have $4,333.33 in our portfolio now (see figure 3.3).

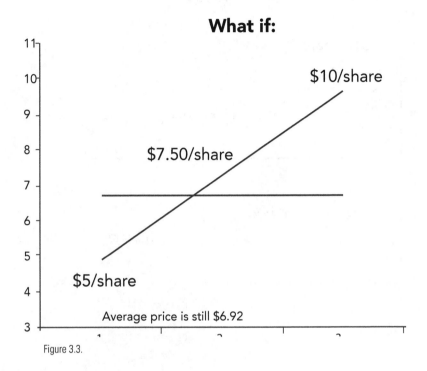

Figure 3.3.

Now, let's look at yet another scenario: same fund, same three prices, different order. The cost per share went from $10 to $7.50 to $5 per share. So again, we have the same average price. And again, we put in $3,000, but now, at $5 per share at year three, our account is worth only $2,166.67. But here's how dollar cost averaging protects us. If we had invested all $3,000 at $10 per share in year one, we would have lost even more money. Because the price per share went from $10 to $5 per share, with the lump-sum, buy-and-hold method, we would only have $1,500.00 left in our portfolio instead of the $2,166.67 we get with dollar cost averaging (see figure 3.4).

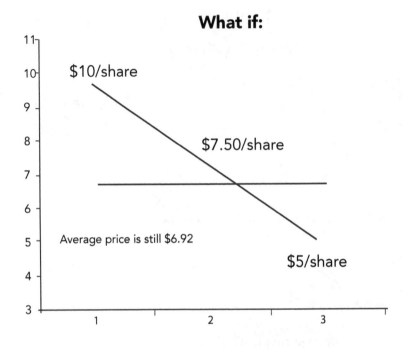

Figure 3.4.

Let's go to a final example. The price per share goes from $10 to $7.50 to $5 to zero. How much do we have now? Zero. That's right: zero. If the price of the fund goes down to zero per share, we might end up with a lot of shares, but their value is still zero (see figure 3.5). So even with dollar cost averaging, there is still risk. The possibility always exists that we could buy WorldCom or Enron or other stocks that go bankrupt and lose everything, even with dollar cost averaging. Usually, however, a mutual fund is sufficiently diversified to prevent the likelihood that all the companies represented in the fund will go bankrupt at the same time.

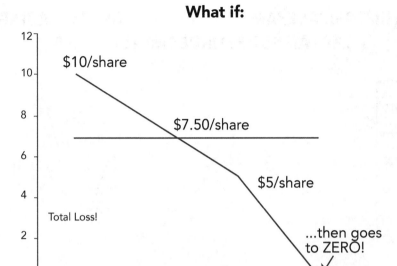

What if:

Figure 3.5.

In a perfect world, if we were paid all of our income in one lump sum instead of having to earn it little by little over the course of our working lives, and we knew the market would go up, we would do better to invest in the market immediately. But since we can't have our income now, and we don't know how the market will fare, dollar cost averaging gives us an edge if the market temporarily crashes.

Dollar cost averaging is a starting point for investing. It is a "one-rule" system that you can use alone, without any other system, to pick a fund or a basket of funds. You can also use it with another type of investment system as long as you maintain consistency with dollar cost averaging and you respect the other system's exit strategies. The following graph shows a back-tested example. For this example, I use historical data on a mutual fund that has been available to the general public.

A HISTORICAL EXAMPLE OF DOLLAR COST AVERAGING INTO AN S&P 500 INDEX MUTUAL FUND

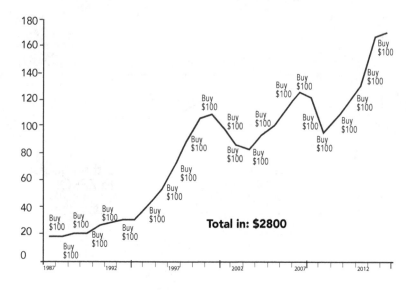

Figure 3.6.

Let's say we have a mutual fund comprised of stocks from the S&P 500 index, which is a highly followed stock index fund. In fact, Vanguard has such a fund, ticker symbol VFINX; it's data is what is used in this back-tested example. If we had started to invest in this fund in 1987, and we had bought $100 worth of shares per year, every year, and reinvested all dividends, we would have invested in this fund for 28 years (1987–2014). Obviously, every year, stocks go up and stocks go down. So let's assume we were the unluckiest investors in the world and bought shares when the stock prices were at their highest for the year. Our average price over 28 years would have been $48.85. Our total return would have been $9,703.23, which represents a 7.7 percent annualized gain (see figure 3.7).

POSSIBLE OUTCOMES OF DOLLAR COST AVERAGING INTO AN S&P 500 INDEX MUTUAL FUND

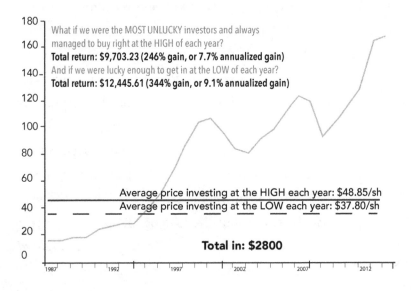

What if we were the MOST UNLUCKY investors and always managed to buy right at the HIGH of each year?
Total return: $9,703.23 (246% gain, or 7.7% annualized gain)
And if we were lucky enough to get in at the LOW of each year?
Total return: $12,445.61 (344% gain, or 9.1% annualized gain)

Average price investing at the HIGH each year: $48.85/sh
Average price investing at the LOW each year: $37.80/sh

Total in: $2800

Figure 3.7.

Now, let's say we were the luckiest investors of all time, and every year, we happened to buy when the market was at its lowest. Our average share price becomes $37.80 per share with an ending total of $12,445.61, or a 9.1 percent annualized gain. So, based on this one example, we can learn several lessons:

1. Even if we used the same system, depending on the time of year or how lucky we were during that year, our returns would vary. In the previous example, they varied between 7.7 percent per year and 9.1 percent per year.

2. Even though the difference looks small, it actually makes a huge impact on our total returns over the long term. When interest is compounded, small differences mean a lot over time.

3. This is why, if you work with a money manager, you need to be very careful about the fees charged because a 1.5 percent fee can cut into your savings over time.

4. Be careful if your fund manager gives you the "average return" of a fund. What some managers want to give you is a *mathematical average*. In other words, if the fund rose by 50 percent in the first year and dropped by 50 percent in the second year, the mathematical average is zero. But in reality, if your fund goes up 50 percent and then goes down 50 percent, you have actually lost 25 percent (100 up 50 percent = 150; 150 down 50 percent = 75; 75 = 100 less 25 percent). That's an annualized *loss* of 13.4 percent per year. Be careful about those two words: *average* and *annualized*. If an *average* gain is offered, ask for clarification.

5. My next point here is the importance of starting early. Even if you only made 7.7 percent on average and you started at 18 years of age, by contributing $5 a day for 50 years until age 68, you would end up with a million dollars ($1,018,071.50). Even small investments pay off when they are made consistently over time. To be fair, a lot of inflation must be taken into account over a period of 50 years. Fifty years ago, $5 represented a lot of money, considering that in 1965 a McDonald's hamburger cost only 18 cents. But then again, even with inflation, one million dollars is still a lot of money.

Here's another historic possibility. Let's say we started late, after the market had gone up, and we started to invest right before the crash of 2000.

POSSIBLE DOLLAR COST AVERAGING STARTING AT THE PEAK OF YEAR 2000

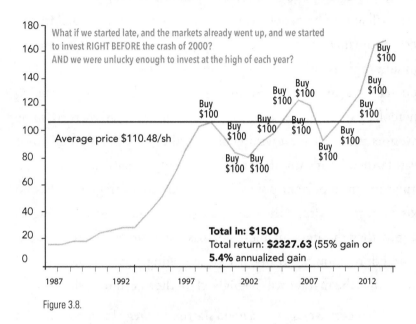

Figure 3.8.

To top it off, we were unlucky enough to invest at the high of each year. So for 15 years, we put in $100 per year for a total of $1,500. Our total return in this example is $2,327.63. That's a 55 percent gain or 5.4 percent annualized gain. So, even though we've had two bear markets since 2000, we still made money (see figure 3.8 above). Remember in this example, our average price is relatively high (coincidentally, around the same price as the peak of 2000), and we would lose money if another bear market came along and pushed prices below the average price.

Dollar cost averaging may or may not be better than a lump sum buy-and-hold. It all depends on factors such as when you start and where the final price is in relationship to your average price. If you have no other system, dollar cost averaging is a good basic strategy to start with. But any system requires discipline, which means following rules. Dollar cost averaging has only one rule: invest consistent amounts at equal periodic intervals. It should be easy to stick to, but there will always be people who decide to skip their periodic deposit because the market seems to be peaking or decide to deposit a greater amount than usual because they think the market is going up. Once you start playing games like that, you're not dollar cost averaging anymore. For instance, toward the end of the bear market, some investors tried to sell everything because the market was going down even farther. That's not dollar cost averaging. That's exiting. And it brings up an important point about dollar cost averaging. It has no exit strategy. In effect, the exit strategy for dollar cost averaging is, simply, that the investor retires or has some urgent financial need to withdraw money. So dollar cost averaging investors hope—and pray—that the market will be high when they need to cash out.

Dollar cost averaging is a good starting strategy for someone who has never invested before and whose account is not complex enough to need a consistent exit strategy. It is a system you can use without a broker. There are mutual funds that will accept initial deposits for as little as $50, as long as you sign up for regular automated periodic investments. Otherwise, they have a minimum requirement of anywhere from $1,000 to $10,000. Just be sure you read the mutual fund's prospectus and talk to its representatives carefully about whether or not there are minimum holding periods. If there are, make sure you know what they are and what the penalties are. If you know nothing else about investing, start here. If and when you discover or develop a better system of investing, you can always close out your old system and convert to the new one. Again, keep in mind that the one rule in using the dollar cost averaging system is consistency. If you're not consistent, you're not dollar cost averaging.

It's that simple. If you change the periodic intervals, skip periods, change the amount you put in, take things out, or change the funds, you're going to distort your model.

This begs the question of what happens if you don't follow the model. As we've seen, it's already hard enough trying to forecast how much of a return you're going to make even if you follow the strategy. It's very difficult to calculate how much you would be hurt by changing the model. The only acceptable change you could make would be to move to a whole new system of investing. In that case, go ahead and consistently follow that strategy on a disciplined basis. You don't have to be stuck with dollar cost averaging forever. You can change it as long as you're changing to a new system. But remember that a good investment system needs an exit strategy. By adding the one rule of an exit strategy, we can improve on the dollar cost averaging system, and that's the basis of our next chapter.

TAKEAWAYS:

Having a plan, even a simple one-rule plan such as dollar cost averaging, gives you an edge over investors who have no plan. Dollar cost averaging works because it forces you to buy more shares when prices are low and fewer shares when prices are high, a concept that is often counterintuitive.

CHAPTER 4

THE 20-MONTH MOVING AVERAGE: ADDING AN EXIT STRATEGY

The 20-month moving average system basically adds an exit strategy to the dollar cost averaging system. Here's how it works: Plot the average price of a fund for the last 20 months. Let's use, for example, a mutual fund (ticker VFINX) that tracks the S&P 500 index again. We plot on a graph the average price for the last 20 months (see figure 4.1 on next page).

When we do this, what we see is that sometimes the index is above the 20-month moving average and sometimes it's below the 20-month moving average. The graph in figure 4.1 shows that when the index is above this magic line, the 20-month moving average, the market tends to go up. Once it crosses below the 20-month moving average, the market tends to go down. So based on this observation,

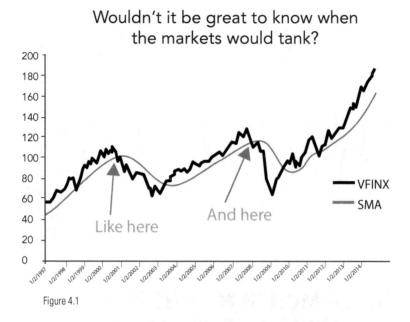

Figure 4.1

the one exit strategy rule is when the market goes below this line, we get out of it. The corollary is when the market goes above this line, it's relatively safe to be in the market.

In order to work, this system requires the discipline to diligently check the monthly average, once a month, every month. This doesn't necessarily mean you're going to trade every month. Over the last 17 years, you may have made just six trades, but you do have to check the graph every month. In the month when your fund goes below the 20-month moving average line, you are going to sell. And in the month when it crosses back up above the 20-month moving average, you are going to buy. You can check it in less than a minute on free websites such as bigcharts.com or stockcharts.com. I've had colleagues time me; it takes me all of 40 seconds to do my monthly check.

Looking at the graph in figure 4.1, the 20-month moving average is simply the average of the last 20 months' worth of prices. When the jagged line of the S&P 500 index drops below the smooth line of the 20-month moving average, the market is likely going down. Every day, every month, the market can go up and the market can go down, but as long as the S&P 500 index stays above that 20-month moving average, the general trend is likely to continue up. When it's below that line, the general trend of the market is to continue going down.

So, let's say you buy an index fund that tracks the S&P 500 index. For our example, I'll use the Vanguard 500 Index, ticker symbol VFINX. When that fund goes down below the 20-month moving average, you sell. You sell the whole fund, cashing out in the month it goes down. If you keep it in cash, when the graph goes above the 20-month moving average, you buy into the VFINX again. If you look at figure 4.2 below, the solid black line represents buying and holding VFINX fund shares and reinvesting the dividends. The grey dashed line represents your cash sale of VFINX shares and your repurchase of VFINX shares when the fund price crosses the 20-month moving average. You can see that by doing that, you will improve your overall return. For example, 21 years of buying and holding shares and reinvesting the dividends, from January 3, 1994, to December 31, 2014, would have produced a gain of 546.98 percent, or an annualized return of 9.3 percent. Had you sold below the 20-month moving average and bought above, the model would have produced a gain of 852.58 percent or an annualized return of 11.3 percent.

COMPARE BUYING-AND-HOLDING TO ACTING ON THE 20-MONTH MOVING AVERAGE

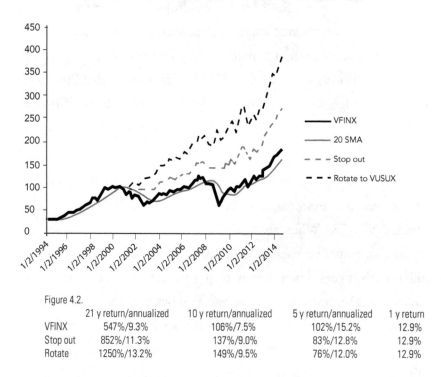

Figure 4.2.

	21 y return/annualized	10 y return/annualized	5 y return/annualized	1 y return
VFINX	547%/9.3%	106%/7.5%	102%/15.2%	12.9%
Stop out	852%/11.3%	137%/9.0%	83%/12.8%	12.9%
Rotate	1250%/13.2%	149%/9.5%	76%/12.0%	12.9%

Let's say that instead of just selling the index fund and going to cash, you sold the index fund and bought a bond fund. For this example, I used the Vanguard Long-Term Treasury Fund, ticker symbol VUSUX. That's the black dotted line in figure 4.2, producing a gain of 1,250.45 percent or a 13.2 percent annualized return. Notice how the black dotted line tends to go up when the solid black line is below the 20-month moving average.

Why do bonds go up when the stocks are not doing as well? Stocks and bonds are not well correlated. Sometimes stocks and bonds do go up together, but in general, if stocks go down, people have a tendency to flock to something safer, such as bonds, and vice versa. This tendency is the basis of modern portfolio theory (MPT), which is translated into the pie chart mantra of "We need to put 70 percent in stocks and 30 percent in bonds, or 60 percent in stocks and 40 percent in bonds, to be well diversified, because we can never predict when stocks will crash or bonds will crash." But if you look over the last 21 years, for at least six of those years, or approximately 30 percent of the time, this model has been in bonds, and 70 percent of the time, it's been in stocks. The system is diversified over time, not diversified at the same time.

Notice how only a few percentage points can make a difference over the long term. For instance, waiting out the big bear markets by sitting on cash increased your annualized gains by "only" 2 percent— from 9.3 percent to 11.3 percent. But it resulted in a 56 percent greater overall gain over 21 years; the account was 47 percent larger at the end of 21 years. By going into bonds during bear markets, you boosted your returns by almost 4 percent, from 9.3 percent annualized gains to 13.2 percent annualized gains, which would have more than doubled your account after 21 years.

This example also illustrates the power of the rule of 72, which states that the amount of time it takes to double an account is roughly equivalent to 72 years divided by the annualized percentage. For instance, at a growth rate of 9.3 percent, it takes 7.8 years (roughly 8 years) to double in size; at a growth rate of 13.2 percent, it takes 5.6 years (roughly 6 years). Over a period of 21 years, this really adds up.

The 20-month moving average is a simple system. It has only two rules.

1. Calculate the 20-month moving average monthly.
2. If the fund price is above the 20-month moving average, you stay in. Otherwise, you get out.

It's an example of a simple system with an exit strategy. The system works well for anyone who doesn't want to bother with looking at the market more than once a month. But you *must* look at it once a month because, just as you don't want to look at it too often, you also don't want to let it go too long. If the market happens to crash during those few months you've decided to not look at your portfolio, you can get wiped out. And the whole point of using this system is to prevent those larger crashes.

One of the downsides to the system is that it is technically possible for stocks and bonds to go down together. However, they don't usually do so for the long term. If they do go down together for the long term, we would probably encounter a large national or global economic problem, and the value of our portfolio would be the least of our problems.

Another downside to this system is that the stock price may be below the 20-month moving average during one month and we'd sell the stocks, but the next month, the stock price may be above the 20-month moving average and we'd buy more stocks. This short-term selling and buying is exactly what happened in 2010 and is called a whipsaw. Whipsaws chew into our returns because of transaction costs and because we most likely sold lower than we bought back. Furthermore, a whipsaw-triggered sell would also create a taxable event. Fortunately, using moving averages based on longer time periods makes whipsaws rare. While most conventional traders use 50-day or 200-day moving averages, 20-month moving averages have demonstrated only one whipsaw in the last 21 years for the S&P 500 index. Medicine is a balance between art and science, and investing is also a balancing act: the longer a moving average, the fewer the whipsaws, but the more you lose before you're stopped out.

The shorter the moving average, the more whipsaws damage your account before a legitimate market change occurs.

The most important point about using the 20-month moving average is that you have to remember to do it every month. Trying the system out is like trying a new habit. If you make a new year's resolution to try jogging every couple of days, you aren't going to actually lose weight or derive any other health benefits unless you follow through and do it faithfully throughout the year. But how many people successfully follow through on their new year's resolutions? It might help you to tie your monthly portfolio check to something else you do monthly, such as paying your bills, to ensure that you follow through diligently. I look forward to the end of each month to check on how my account is performing. It's like losing weight: if you're successful, each time you weigh yourself, you get that sense of elation from progress, so you weigh yourself more regularly. The same is true of this monthly investing ritual. While your account in any one month could go up or down, you see real progress when you look back as little as a year at how much your account was worth. Since, most of the time, we're not actually placing a trade, it only takes about 40 seconds to do a check. It may take someone who is not as familiar with the system five minutes to check. If you are making a trade, it's a matter of logging into your accounts and placing the trade, which might take a few more minutes, depending on which platform you use. But overall, it's not a big time commitment.

Another weakness of the 20-month moving average system is that some people tend to change their plan when their money is on the line. If they intended to trade with a system or invest with a system but then change the system in midcourse, it's no longer a system. In other words, if they start using one system and later read or hear about a different system based on some other rule and they switch to that system instead, they break the system. In fact, they no longer even have a system. The whole point of the 20-month moving average system is to have a plan going in and out and to stick with it. Recognize that we only think clearly when our capital is not invested. We make our best plans before we commit a single dollar. Once we commit, our emotions, such as fear and greed, take over. Emotions can sabotage even a simple, robust system because they will seduce you away from following the system. Plan your exit before you commit a single dollar.

Markets go up and down, so it's hard to predict from one year to the next how well you'd do over 20 years or even one year. Past performance does not guarantee future results. But with the 20-month moving average strategy, at least we know that, for the long term, we can mitigate the large bear markets significantly. If the system puts you in stocks, but the news reports terrorist attacks, wars, Russian invasions, rampant crime, Ebola, and the market taking a dive today, does it mean it's not working? No, it means that it's not time to get out of stocks yet if it's not yet the end of the month and if the stocks are still above the 20-month moving average. If the system has you out of stocks, does that mean it's not working? No, it means you're not supposed to be in stocks during this phase. There's often anxiety about entering an already-high market. How do we know we're not investing at the top? Let the system tell you when it is time to get in and when it is time to get out. This way, if you lose something, it won't be that much. It will be a recoverable amount. It won't be a 50 percent drop, which obliges you to make 100 percent to recoup your losses.

Another point about moving averages is that websites may offer you a choice of different types of moving averages. A simple moving average is calculated by adding together the closing prices of the stock for the last few time periods and dividing that total by that same number of time periods. For a 20-month moving average, you take the closing prices of the last 20 months, add them together, and divide by 20. A simple moving average is often abbreviated as SMA. To calculate an exponential, or weighted, 20-month moving average, you take the last month's moving average value, multiply it by 19/20, and add 1/20th of today's price to that average. The advantage to the exponential or weighted moving average is this: let's say that, one day, a stock gaps up or gaps down, way out of normal range. Suddenly, your whole 20-month moving average jumps. Not only does it jump, but 20 months later, it will jump again when that data point is no longer counted. A weighted moving average smoothes out curves like that. It takes into account the entire data history instead of just the last 20 months (or last 20 time periods). With that said, I still advocate using the simple 20-month moving average. Using a time period this long, you don't see the S&P 500 index gap as much. I advocate using this system because anyone with a spreadsheet can calculate it or use one of the many readily available resources.

Going back to figure 4.1, the graph seems to indicate we're not selling at the high point but rather, when the market starts to go down *after* reaching the high point. Similarly, we're buying only after the fund has been going up for months after the low of the market. This seems to go against the rule of buy low, sell high. The problem with buying low and selling high is knowing when the fund is at a low or at a high. We can't tell the high was reached until the fund starts to seriously deviate away from the high. In fact, when we see these multiyear growth curves, it's often possible to look at a yearly chart, buy high, and then, sell higher. After holding our shares past the high, we stay with the fund until it starts to go down enough for the system to trigger a sell signal. You can only truly see the high in retrospect, but with this SMA system, you are selling very close to it.

Another beautiful thing about the 20-month moving average system is that if you find a better strategy, it's simple to exit this system any time you want, keeping in mind that once you stop using the system, you completely stop using it. Don't try to combine systems. You can dollar-cost-average into this system just as you can dollar-cost-average into any other system. Other than that, once you start to add rules or replace rules or disregard rules, you're no longer following the system. Before switching to a new system, it would be highly advisable to at least back-test it to make sure it does just as well, if not better, than the 20-month moving average system.

TAKEAWAYS:

The 20-month moving average system is a simple two-rule system complete with an exit strategy. Its strengths are that it only takes a few minutes each month to manage; it helps avoid large losses; and if you use this system in conjunction with a bond fund, it diversifies over time dynamically (not pie-chart statically) while increasing overall returns beyond what the stocks or bonds do by themselves. Its weaknesses are 1) it requires the discipline to do it every month, even if, most of the time, you're not trading, and 2) yes, the entire economy could crash, in which case this system would crash too.

THE MONTHLY ROTATION INVESTMENT SYSTEM: BACKGROUND

In chapter 3, we covered a one-rule "system": dollar cost averaging. In chapter 4, we covered a two-rule system—the 20-month moving average—and how flipping between two asset classes can mitigate risk and boost overall performance. Now I want to introduce you to a way we can modify and expand upon the diversification concept of these systems with my MRI (Monthly Rotation Investment) system.

The MRI builds on the two-fund strategy of the 20-month moving average system. The MRI dynamically rotates between funds and is not limited to just two asset classes or two funds. I first became aware of a variation of this system through a financial newsletter I read back in 1995. At that time the system used 33 Fidelity Select

Sector funds, and you started by buying the top four funds of the week. Fidelity Select Funds required a minimum investment of $2,500 each, at the time. I didn't have enough money at that time to have four positions at $2,500 each. I could only start with one, funded by my IRA account.

The publisher discontinued the newsletter several years later. To continue using that system, I had to look up the prices of 33 funds, correcting for dividends, subtracting, and ranking them every month, which ate up a huge chunk of my time. The reason I had subscribed to the newsletter was to not have to spend my time doing that research. When they discontinued the newsletter, I complained so vociferously that the CEO called to mollify me. He told me he had been using a software program called Investor's Fast Track (www. fasttrack.net) to do the calculations. I was able to get ahold of the software, which was not an easy piece of software to learn to use. It was written in the 1990s in DOS 3.1, but once I had familiarized myself with it, I found I could experiment easily on various funds and models.

One way I modified the model to get around the annoying 31-day-minimum hold time for Fidelity Select funds was to experiment with something relatively new, available to investors: exchange traded funds (ETFs), which are, basically, mutual funds with shares that trade on the open market like stocks—no minimum holding times, no waiting until the end of the day or the next day to see how my order was filled, and lower expenses, and it seemed as if more variety and innovative funds were being introduced every year.

A note about the differences between mutual funds and ETFs: Traditionally, mutual funds are companies (or "funds") that invest in stocks, bonds, or other securities. These funds are, typically, large compared to the average investor's holdings, but they enable investors to buy many positions of securities at the same time. The price of stock in the S&P 500 index ranges between $17 per share and $530 per share, as of this writing. The average investor is not able to buy shares in all 500 stocks of the index but can buy shares in a mutual fund that buys shares in all 500 stocks. Mutual funds, typically, recalculate the total net worth of the fund at the end of the day, and any purchases or redemptions of these funds are based on that end-of-day calculation. Investors purchasing funds are, in effect, buying shares directly from the mutual fund itself and can easily do so through most brokerages. The fund is identified by its unique ticker symbol (every stock and security has a unique identifier, such as a ticker symbol or CUSIP number). A mutual fund's ticker symbol is usually a five-letter symbol ending in X. For instance, the Vanguard S&P 500 Index, often used in this book as an example, has the ticker symbol VFINX.

Exchange-traded funds are similar to the mutual fund in concept. ETFs are also funds that buy a portfolio of stocks or other securities, only these funds are closed-ended. This means there are only so many shares of these funds (they're not created or destroyed as investors purchase or redeem shares), so they can be bought and sold on the stock exchanges just like shares of stock of any other company. Typically, these ETFs' ticker symbols are two to four characters in length, without a requirement to use any one character. For instance, an example of an ETF that buys the S&P 500 index of stocks is the SPDR S&P 500 ETF, ticker symbol SPY.

Remember that no matter how many assets a fund or ETF buys and holds, each fund or ETF is specialized. A stock fund only holds stocks; a bond fund only holds bonds, and so on. There are mixed funds that hold a fixed percentage of stocks versus bonds, and there are superspecialized sector funds that invest only in oil stocks, or technology stocks, or whatever sector of the universe of stocks are available. Holdings can be static. In other words, they may hold a definite fixed ratio of assets, or holdings can be dynamic, meaning that fund managers have the discretion to change the composition of the funds within the parameters of the fund. For simplicity and efficiency, we will use index funds in our investment models.

Another innovation that helped me during the 2000s was a short fund. What's a "short fund"? A typical fund buys stocks, and when the stock market goes up, your funds go up. An inverse fund, or a short fund, tries to do the opposite of what the stock market is doing. If the market is up, the inverse fund is down. And here we have the key to the MRI strategy: the inverse fund.

A note about shorting for those readers who may not understand what it means to "short" a stock. Buying a stock and selling it later involves two transactions: one to buy and one to sell. Profit or loss is based on the buying price and the selling price (minus any commissions and fees). Shorting a stock involves first borrowing stock from the broker/dealer, selling it, and then buying back shares when shares are (hopefully) cheaper, thereby making a profit. There is still a buy transaction and a sell transaction but in a different order, and losses are possible, since stocks can rise after you sell short. You can see how, if you buy a stock, every time the stock goes up $1, the value of your portfolio goes up $1 times the number of shares you own. Conversely, if you short a stock, every time the stock goes up $1, the value of your portfolio goes *down* $1 times the number of shares you're short. Keeping track of short shares of stock may be tricky for the inexperienced investor, and shorting stock is not allowed in tax-advantaged retirement accounts. A short, or inverse mutual fund, solves both the problem of tracking and the problem of direct shorting by allowing the investor to buy shares of the inverse fund when the investor thinks the market will go down.

Traditional investing, using diversification models using modern portfolio theory, usually incorporates negative beta to mitigate risk of the pie chart. Beta is a measure of the performance of one stock, or other equity, compared to another. MPT advocates including a fund that can do the opposite of what your main fund does for diversification purposes. The strength (and weakness) of modern portfolio theory is to decrease losses (and gains) through diversification. The less correlated the assets (beta closer to 0 than 1), the less likely they will all head down (or up) at the same time. In theory, an asset that has negative beta (goes up when your main fund goes down) would provide stronger protection against market downturns than an asset that has a more neutral beta. Traditionally, bonds have provided the negative beta fund to offset the risk of stocks. However, the beta correlation between stocks and bonds has not been strong. For modern portfolio theory, that's actually a good thing since modern portfolio theory relies on both stocks and bonds to sometimes go up together. It made sense to me that if you could use the inverse fund to not just mitigate bear markets but also make money during bear markets, there must be a way to use that with a sector rotation system to really boost returns. I wanted an inverse fund to do more than just balance the other fund. I wanted to use it to make money.

From 1995 to the early 2000s, I did a variation of the sector rotation system. Every week a newsletter was published that listed and ranked the top-performing Fidelity sector funds for the week. I had to buy the top four funds, and if one of those funds dropped below the top ten funds, I had to sell that fund and buy the top fund. At that time, the system made sense since, in theory, there was always a bull market in some sector of the economy or other. And in fact, the model worked well; it was one of my investing systems that survived the bear market of 2000–2002 with relatively small losses, and since it was a mutual-fund-only system, I used it in my IRA and 401(k) accounts. During the 2000s, I improved on the success of the US-only system by investing in 33 different foreign funds on the assumption that there's always a bull market somewhere in the world. I rotated them every month. That method worked really well for me until 2007 when all the markets across the world went down.

It was at this time of crisis that I realized that the model I was back-testing, the one that included the inverse fund, was actually doing better than my 33 foreign fund system. In fact, with the back-testing system, I found that if I just added one extra fund—namely, the emerging markets fund—I could help detect and deal with those bear markets.

I went down from the complicated 33-fund system to a more manageable three-fund system.

MRI APPLIED TO THREE FUNDS

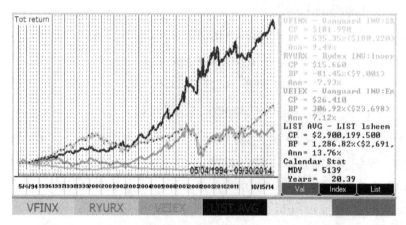

Figure 5.1. These are the results of ranking and rotating a quarter of a portfolio between the three funds VFINX, RYURX, and VEIEX; software from www.fasttrack.net.

Figure 5.1 shows a model of how the MRI line (the solid black line) gives you a 13.76 percent annualized return while smoothing out when the market drops. But there are still weaknesses because, every month, we actively adjust, and therefore the system is prone to whipsaws. That's why, when the market is rip-roaring, going higher and higher every month but in a choppy way (up one month, down another), this system doesn't do well. But the upside is that when the market crashes, this system doesn't crash nearly as much. One of the reasons I built this system was for safety, especially after 2004.

Conventional wisdom says that you should have a set ratio of asset classes in your portfolio, represented graphically by a pie chart (see figure 5.2), and you should rebalance your portfolio annually, or maybe semi-annually or quarterly. For example, if you have 60 percent of your assets in stocks and 40 percent in bonds, and in one year the stocks did so much better than the bonds that you now have 70 percent in stocks versus 30 percent in bonds, you'd sell off enough stock and buy enough bonds to get your portfolio back to 60 percent stock/40 percent bonds.

CONVENTIONAL PIE CHART INVESTING

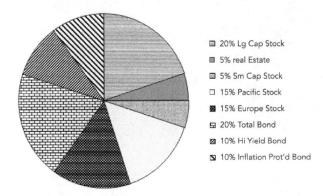

- 20% Lg Cap Stock
- 5% real Estate
- 5% Sm Cap Stock
- 15% Pacific Stock
- 15% Europe Stock
- 20% Total Bond
- 10% Hi Yield Bond
- 10% Inflation Prot'd Bond

Figure 5.2. This figure is a graphic representation of how a money manager invests by diversifying funds in various asset classes and then, rebalancing, either quarterly or yearly. In this case, the money manager touts a 60 percent stock/40 percent bond mix (real estate in the form of a REIT is, technically, a stock) that, by virtue of its diversification, is sold as intelligently robust.

PIE CHART INVESTING: ANOTHER VIEW

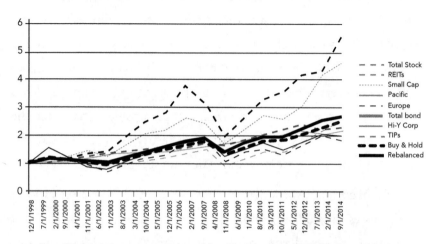

Figure 5.3. A typical money manager's portfolio will consist of a combination of mutual funds representing various asset classes, such as large US company stocks, small US company stocks, overseas stocks, real estate, and several types of bonds. In this example, 60 percent of the holdings are in stocks and real estate and 40 percent are in bonds, similar in proportion to the pie chart in figure 5.2. The chart shows how each individual component fared over 16 years. The model of just buying the components of the pie chart and not touching the account for 16 years is represented by the dashed black line, which returns 153.1 percent, or 5.89 percent per year, annualized. If rebalanced quarterly, the returns on the model would improve, as represented by the solid black line, which returns 174.1 percent, or 6.36 percent per year, annualized. Point 1: A small percentage difference (half a percent per year) results in a portfolio that is 8 percent larger over a period of 15 years. Time is your friend, and every little bit counts. Point 2: Although the pie chart (the black solid or dashed lines) never does as badly as the worst fund of the mix, it never does as well or better than the best fund of the mix. With pie chart investing, at best, you earn the average of the mix.

THE TRADITIONAL ARGUMENT FOR PIE CHART INVESTING

1999	2000	2001	2002	2003	2004	2005	2006	2007	2008	2009	2010	2011	2012	2013	2014
Pacific Stock 57.1%	Real Estate 26.2%	Sm Cap Stock 14.0%	Inflation Prot Bond 11.9%	Pacific Stock 40.3%	Real Estate 30.8%	Pacific Stock 22.5%	Real Estate 35.1%	Europe Stock 13.8%	Total Bond 5.2%	Hi Yield Bond 39.2%	Real Estate 28.3%	Inflation Prot Bond 13.2%	Europe Stock 20.8%	Sm Cap Stock 36.4%	Real Estate 30.1%
Lg Cap Stock 23.8%	Sm Cap Stock 22.0%	Real Estate 12.4%	Total Bond 8.5%	Europe Stock 38.7%	Sm Cap Stock 23.6%	Real Estate 11.9%	Europe Stock 33.5%	Inflation Prot Bond 11.6%	Inflation Prot Bond (2.9%)	Europe Stock 31.9%	Sm Cap Stock 24.8%	Real Estate 8.4%	Sm Cap Stock 18.5%	Lg Cap Stock 33.3%	Lg Cap Stock 12.4%
Europe Stock 16.7%	Total Bond 11.5%	Total Bond 8.4%	Real Estate 3.7%	Sm Cap Stock 37.2%	Europe Stock 20.9%	Europe Stock 9.2%	Sm Cap Stock 19.3%	Total Bond 6.9%	Hi Yield Bond (21.2%)	Sm Cap Stock 30.3%	Lg Cap Stock 17.1%	Total Bond 7.6%	Real Estate 17.5%	Europe Stock 24.7%	Sm Cap Stock 10.4%
Sm Cap Stock 3.3%	Inflation Prot Bond 11.5%	Inflation Prot Bond 5.3%	Hi Yield Bond 1.2%	Real Estate 35.7%	Pacific Stock 19.0%	Sm Cap Stock 6.1%	Lg Cap Stock 15.5%	Lg Cap Stock 5.5%	Sm Cap Stock (32.1%)	Real Estate 29.4%	Pacific Stock 15.7%	Hi Yield Bond 7.2%	Lg Cap Stock 16.3%	Pacific Stock 17.4%	Total Bond 5.7%
Hi Yield Bond 2.9%	Hi Yield Bond (0.8%)	Hi Yield Bond 2.9%	Pacific Stock (7.4%)	Lg Cap Stock 31.4%	Lg Cap Stock 12.5%	Lg Cap Stock 6.0%	Pacific Stock 12.0%	Pacific Stock 4.8%	Pacific Stock (34.3%)	Lg Cap Stock 28.7%	Hi Yield Bond 11.8%	Lg Cap Stock 1.0%	Pacific Stock 15.4%	Hi Yield Bond 4.6%	Hi Yield Bond 4.6%
Total Bond (0.8%)	Europe Stock (8.2%)	Lg Cap Stock (11.0%)	Sm Cap Stock (14.3%)	Hi Yield Bond 15.7%	Hi Yield Bond 8.8%	Inflation Prot Bond 2.6%	Hi Yield Bond 8.5%	Hi Yield Bond 2.0%	Lg Cap Stock (37.0%)	Pacific Stock 21.2%	Total Bond 6.3%	Sm Cap Stock (4.1%)	Hi Yield Bond 14.5%	Real Estate 2.3%	Inflation Prot Bond 3.9%
Inflation Prot Bond (0.8%)	Lg Cap Stock (10.6%)	Europe Stock (20.3%)	Europe Stock (18.0%)	Inflation Prot Bond 7.3%	Inflation Prot Bond 8.3%	Hi Yield Bond 2.5%	Total Bond 4.4%	Sm Cap Stock (7.1%)	Real Estate (37.1%)	Inflation Prot Bond 10.8%	Inflation Prot Bond 6.2%	Europe Stock (11.5%)	Inflation Prot Bond 6.8%	Total Bond (2.2%)	Pacific Stock (4.7%)
Real Estate (4.0%)	Pacific Stock (25.7%)	Pacific Stock (26.4%)	Lg Cap Stock (21.0%)	Total Bond 3.9%	Total Bond 4.2%	Total Bond 2.4%	Inflation Prot Bond 0.4%	Real Estate (16.4%)	Europe Stock (44.7%)	Total Bond 5.9%	Europe Stock 5.0%	Pacific Stock (13.9%)	Total Bond 4.1%	Inflation Prot Bond (9.0%)	Europe Stock (6.7%)

Figure 5.4. Here is the theoretical basis of pie chart investing. Money managers will tell you that every year, different asset classes do well, and it is impossible to predict which assets, or funds, will do well during the coming year. In fact, there is a very good likelihood that the fund that did the best this past year will not be the fund that does well next year, hence the need to rebalance.

The strength of the pie chart (see figure 5.3) is that you never do as badly as the worst fund. The corollary is—or perhaps, I should say the weakness is—you'll also never do as well as or better than the best fund. The only risk management system of a pie chart is that it gives you average returns. There is no reason to check the pie chart monthly, which is why most brokers tell you to check it annually. Some money managers claim they're more diligent because they check and rebalance it quarterly rather than annually. And you may be able to outperform a pie chart by a quarter of a percent to half a percent more per year by rebalancing quarterly rather than annually.

If you use the MRI system and check your portfolio monthly, over the long term, it is possible to outperform even the best fund because you are always rotating out of the losers and into the winners (see figure 5.1 on the previous page). If you only check your portfolio quarterly, you won't respond to changing market conditions as fast as the monthly strategy to avoid larger losses as bear markets arise.

When I back-tested the system, I compared the last day of the previous month to the last day of the current month for each month, but you can use any day of the month, as long as you're consistent. What's important is that you use a one-month span. If you check less frequently, your risks are greater and your gains aren't as dramatic because you're not rotating whole hog into the top fund or rotating away from developing bear markets as quickly. On the other hand, you can check more often, but then, the costs of the trades (slippage) and whipsaws will start catching up with you.

Can your money manager do this for you? Yes. Will she do so? Probably not. While there might be unscrupulous managers who are just out to sell the house load funds, I think even the more well-meaning money managers are not experienced with some of these concepts and thus are unwilling to do something they're not familiar with. To be fair, money managers don't want to do something they don't understand, because they want to protect you. "Don't invest in anything you don't understand" is a good rule for money managers too, not just for you, the investor.

There were times when I didn't follow my own rules. I'd check more often and think, "This fund is doing so well, I might as well just pull the trigger and start rotating now" instead of waiting until the end of the month. Or I might encounter some financial news or chart indicator that indicated the market was going to imminently crash in a certain sector, so I got out of it at that point instead of waiting for the monthly calculation. Every single time I tried to jump the gun and do what I thought was right, the system was proven right, and I was proven wrong. The last mistake I made was two years ago. I thought the market was going to go down because so many things were going on in the news and the pundits' technical analysis told me that a market crash was imminent. So I decided to switch out of my VFINX fund into bonds while waiting for the next signal because I was afraid that the market would go down. But I wasn't so confident about the market going down that I bought the inverse fund. Lo and behold, the market didn't crash. It kept going up, and I was sitting with bonds. After the next regularly scheduled monthly calculation, I got back into the VFINX fund, having lost out on a couple of percentage points of gain for not sticking with the system.

Some of my colleagues have commented on my "interesting system," but when I've explained how they can use monthly updates, they often didn't put that information to use with their accounts. Even my dad has questioned me on it. In 2010 and 2011, when the American market was going up, this system was fairly flat. At the time, I was also investing for my dad, who criticized my system because the market was going up and his account was staying flat. I showed him a graph of how the system worked (see figure 5.1, up to year 2011). Once I showed my dad the graph, he felt better. Eight years earlier, I had crashed his account, which was horrible. Now I was showing him a system that made it difficult to crash and could help him to do better than the market in the long run. This is especially important for him now that he is older and retired, as he can't afford to have a bear market hit him at this point in his life. Being able to see the graph calmed him.

Similarly, the performance of the MRI in 2014 lags the bull market of 2014, as of this writing. It is a defensive strategy. But of all the investment systems I've looked at and tried over the past 19 years, this system has been one of the most consistent in detecting and dealing with the larger bear markets. It is the system that I use with my 401(k). I want to share this strategy because it's a system that anyone can use successfully, as we'll see in the next chapter.

TAKEAWAYS:

This chapter has introduced the fundamental components of the MRI strategy (mutual funds, ETFs, inverse funds) as well as the history underlying my MRI system's development and current use as my workhorse investment strategy.

PUTTING THE MRI TO WORK

In chapter 5 we introduced the elements of the MRI system. Now let's go through some examples of how to implement it. We will use mutual funds in the following examples, but in reality, you have the choice of using either a mutual fund or a corresponding ETF, keeping in mind there are pros and cons to using mutual funds and pros and cons to using ETFs.

The funds:

- VFINX (the fund), or SPY (the ETF): track the S&P 500 index
- VEIEX (the fund), or EEM (the ETF): track the MSCI Emerging Markets Index
- RYURX (the fund), or SH (the ETF): the Rydex Inverse S&P 500 Fund

The formula is to rank each fund by how well it performed in the past month; sell the bottom 25 percent of your portfolio and buy the top fund based on the rankings.

How do you calculate the ranking? For purposes of this example, let's say today is 12/31/2014, the last trading day of the month. For VFINX, "today's" price is $189.89. The price on 11/30/2014 (the last trading day of last month) was $191.4, so $189.89/$191.4 = 0.992111. Do this for each fund and make a table:

EXAMPLE MONTHLY CALCULATION

	11/30/2014	12/31/2014	% Return
VFINX/SPY	191.4	189.89	0.992111
VEIEX/EEM	26.75	25.32	0.946542
RYURX/SH	14.8	14.81	1.000676

Figure 6.1. This is a sample calculation of % return of the mutual funds used in MRI for ranking purposes

Based on the table above (figure 6.1), we would sell the bottom 25 percent of our portfolio and use those funds to buy RYURX/SH. For instance, if our portfolio were worth $100,000, 25 percent of our portfolio would be $25,000. If we currently hold VEIEX/EEM, we would sell up to $25,000 of VEIEX/EEM to buy RYURX/SH. If we did not have enough VEIEX/EEM, we would sell all we had and then sell enough VFINX/SPY until we had sold a total of $25,000. Then, we would use the funds to buy RYURX/SH. If we did not have enough VEIEX/EEM or VFINX/PY to sell, well, congratulations, we are now 100 percent in RYURX/SH, the fund in the dominant trend. Next month, and every month after that, lather, rinse, repeat.

Calculate and rank the new dominant fund and rotate 25 percent of your portfolio into that fund.

Note that with the MRI system, if the system indicates the same dominant fund for four months in a row, it is possible to be 100 percent in only one fund. The fact that we can be 100 percent in any one fund will blow the mind of anyone who is brainwashed into thinking we must be diversified at all times. Note that we are indeed diversified, only our diversification occurs over time, not necessarily all at once. If a strong multimonth trend starts (such as a major bear market) within four months, we will be rotated out of losing funds and into the dominant fund.

One weakness of the MRI system is that every time you make a trade, you incur costs. Aside from commissions (a typical discount broker may charge about $9 per trade, with one buy trade and one sell trade per month, which is a cost of $18/month), there is slippage (a stock or ETF is often quoted as a pair of prices: the lower "bid" price and the higher "ask" price. Retail investors can only buy at the higher "ask" price and sell at the lower "bid" price, which is how brokers and market makers make their living), and then, there is the cost of a whipsaw.

As I mentioned earlier, a whipsaw happens when you sell one ETF one month and buy it again the next. Or it can be the opposite, if you buy one ETF one month and sell the next. Presumably, you bought the ETF, originally, because it was going up, but you sold it because it started to go down after you bought it the previous month. True, these little losses help prevent larger losses later on, but whipsaw losses can add up over time. So during times of seemingly robust bull markets (such as 1997–1999 or 2010–2012), the MRI system will not do as well as the benchmark S&P 500 index due to whipsaws between VFINX and VEIEX. However, during the bear markets of 2000–2002 and 2007–2009, when there was a mathematical downtrend, RYURX dominated for months, protecting the portfolio.

Can whipsaws happen when the market is flat? Let's say one month the VFINX fund is up 1 percent, and the RYURX fund is down 1 percent, and the VEIEX is flat. You would sell the RYURX fund and buy the VFINX fund. Then, say, the next month, the RYURX fund goes up 1 percent, and the VFINX fund goes down 1 percent, and the VEIEX fund stays flat. Well, now you're selling the VFINX fund and buying the RYURX fund, so you just made a round trip in two months. If you had bought and held for those two months, you'd be, roughly, flat. But because you bought and sold, you're actually down a little bit. When markets are sideways like this, our MRI system will be relatively flat to slightly down. So it is possible to lose money because of the increased cost of trading with the MRI when markets are going sideways—in other words, when there's no real trend. The MRI system is a defensive strategy in which you automatically rotate out of losers. That's the MRI system's exit strategy.

Here is a more illustrative example, using hypothetical funds: We can compare how buy-hold-and-pray, rebalancing, and MRI work and compare to each other. Let's say we have three funds: TOPX, MEHX, and BADX. For ease of calculation, we'll say we have $90,000, and we put one-third ($30,000) into each fund. So, in the beginning, we have:

$30,000 in TOPX
$30,000 in MEHX
$30,000 in BADX

$90,000 Total

Scenario 1: If, for three months, TOPX goes up 1 percent/month, MEHX does nothing, and BADX goes down 1 percent/month, and we did not adjust:

	Start	Month 1	Month 2	Month 3
TOPX	$30,000	$30,300	$30,603	$30,909
MEHX	$30,000	$30,000	$30,000	$30,000
BADX	$30,000	$29,700	$29,403	$29,109
TOTAL	$90,000	$90,000	$90,006	$90,018

Scenario 2, monthly rebalancing: If, for three months, TOPX goes up 1 percent/month, MEHX does nothing, and BADX goes down 1 percent/month, but we rebalanced every month:

			Month		Month		Month
	Start		1		2		3
TOPX	$30,000		$30,3000		$30,300		$30,300
MEHX	$30,000		$30,000		$30,000		$30,000
BADX	$30,000		$29,700		$29,700		$29,700
TOTAL	$90,000		$90,000		$90,000		$90,000
			V		V		V
TOPX		Rebalance to:$30,000		Rebalance to:$30,000		Rebalance to:$30,000	
MEHX			$30,000		$30,000		$30,000
BADX			$30,000		$30,000		$30,000
TOTAL			$90,000		$90,000		$90,000

Scenario 3, the MRI: If, for three months, TOPX goes up 1 percent/month, MEHX does nothing, and BADX goes down 1 percent/month, but we sell the worst 25 percent of the portfolio and bought the best:

	Start		Month 1		Month 2		Month 3
TOPX	$30,000		$30,3000		$53,328		$76,701
MEHX	$30,000		$30,000		$30,000		$14,514
BADX	$30,000		$29,700		$7,128		$0
TOTAL	$90,000		$90,000		$90,456		$91,215
			V		V		V
TOPX			Rebalance to:$52,800		Rebalance to:$75,942		Rebalance to:$91,215
MEHX			$30,000		$14,514		$0
BADX			$7,200		$0		$0
TOTAL			$90,000		$90,456		$91,215

To summarize, at this point, our running total for three months looks like this:

- Scenario 1 (Buy-hold-and-pray): $90,018/$90,000 = 0.02 percent return in three months.
- Scenario 2 (Rebalance back to pie chart): $90,000/$90,000 = 0.000 percent return in three months.
- Scenario 3 (MRI system): $91,215/$90,000 = 1.35 percent return in three months.

Note that it is possible, with the MRI, to completely rotate into just one fund if that one fund demonstrates consistent multimonth trend dominance.

It is important to understand that each system has both strengths and weaknesses. In this example, the strength of the MRI system is obvious over the alternatives (buy-hold-and-pray, monthly rebalancing) during a distinct TOPX trend. But what if we had the following scenario?

- Month 1: TOPX goes up 1 percent, MEHX stays flat, BADX goes down 1 percent.
- Month 2: TOPX goes *down* 1 percent, MEHX stays flat, BADX goes *up* 1 percent.
- Month 3: TOPX goes up 1 percent, MEHX stays flat, BADX goes down 1 percent.

If we run the numbers, it looks like this:

Scenario 1: Buy-hold-and-pray

	Start	Month 1	Month 2	Month 3
TOPX	$30,000	$30,300	$29,997	$30,297
MEHX	$30,000	$30,000	$30,000	$30,000
BADX	$30,000	$29,700	$29,997	$29,697
TOTAL	$90,000	$90,000	$89,994	$89,994

Scenario 2: Monthly Rebalancing

			Month		Month		Month
	Start		1		2		3
TOPX	$30,000		$30,3000		$29,700		$30,300
MEHX	$30,000		$30,000		$30,000		$30,000
BADX	$30,000		$29,700		$30,300		$29,700
TOTAL	$90,000		$90,000		$90,000		$90,000
			V		V		V
TOPX		Rebalance to:$30,000		Rebalance to:$30,000		Rebalance to:$30,000	
MEHX			$30,000		$30,000		$30,000
BADX			$30,000		$30,000		$30,000
TOTAL			$90,000		$90,000		$90,000

Scenario 3, the MRI:

			Month		Month		Month
	Start		1		2		3
TOPX	$30,000		$30,3000		$52,272		$30,185
MEHX	$30,000		$30,000		$30,000		$30,000
BADX	$30,000		$29,700		$7,272		$29,391
TOTAL	$90,000		$90,000		$89,544		$89,544
			V		V		V
TOPX		Rebalance to:$52,800		Rebalance to:$29,886		Rebalance to:$52,571	
MEHX			$30,000		$30,000		$30,000
BADX			$7,200		$29,658		$6,975
TOTAL			$90,000		$89,544		$89,544

After three months, these are the returns for each system:

- Buy-hold-and-pray: $89,994/$90,000 = (0.007% loss)
- Rebalancing: $90,000/$90,000 = (0.000%)
- MRI: $89,546.28/$90,000 = (0.5% loss)

This hypothetical example illustrates two concepts:

1. The concept of the devastating effects of losses on a portfolio. Remember on a percentage basis, it always takes more to make up for what was lost (11 percent gains make up for 10 percent losses; 33 percent gains make up for 25 percent losses; 100 percent gains make up for 50 percent losses, etc.). In this case, it takes a 1.01 percent gain to make up for a 1 percent loss. This is why an inverse fund tends to drift down compared to its corresponding index, even if there is no significant expense otherwise. This is also why, if we put an inverse fund into the MRI mix, we are only seldom in the inverse fund. The inverse fund serves a strategic purpose to reverse losses only during prolonged bear markets.

2. The concept of whipsaws. In this case, when there are two competing funds that are both relatively flat or going up, one may dominate in one month yet be surpassed in another month. During these times of market indecision, the MRI system will automatically recalibrate each month, resulting in a drag on portfolio performance.

In general, the two strengths of the MRI system (being able to identify and rotate into dominant multimonth trends and being able to rotate out of bear markets and decrease bear market losses) more than compensate for its two weaknesses mentioned above. It is important to understand both the strengths and weaknesses of any investment or investment system before committing a single dollar.

We've so far mentioned two weaknesses of using ETFs: a bid/ask gap in prices and commissions. We should also be cognizant of two other weaknesses that concern those of us who work during market hours. Since ETFs trade like stocks, we need to place trades when the market is open. We can somewhat circumvent this by placing limit orders the night before, but we risk poor or no fills if there are price gaps against us. Also, if we're supposed to rotate from X into Y because X is going down and Y is going up, while the market is open, X is going down even more while Y is going up even more. By the time we confirm a sale of X so we'd know how much money we have to buy, Y has gone up.

If these weaknesses exist with ETFs, why stay away from mutual funds? Mutual fund companies have rules against "frequent trading." Some mutual funds will disallow, freeze, or otherwise penalize investors who buy and sell a fund within a relatively small time window, typically 30 or 60 days. Then, why include mutual funds in this discussion? Mutual funds have been around longer than ETFs; all back-testing in this book has been done on mutual funds for that very reason. These particular mutual funds also have more digits in their prices, enabling more precise calculations for ranking purposes. Some months the mutual funds are so close together comparisons would have to be carried out to the fifth most significant digit. (Notice how, in figure 6.1, the percent return column is carried out to the fifth decimal point. This is not by accident.)

TAKEAWAYS:

As physicians, we are trained to examine patients in a systematic way. When I look at X-rays or a CT scan, I follow algorithms and protocols. I use search patterns. All doctors use organized ways of examining patients, of treating certain diseases, or reviewing data. If you approach investing in the same way you approach medicine, you will be more successful. This is not to say I discount completely the use of intuition, but intuition based on systematic experience with data is more reliable than intuition without data. If you always examine a patient following the same order of steps, it's less likely that you'll miss something and so your intuition is more likely to be accurate. It's the same with stocks. If you approach investing, using a system such as the MRI, your portfolio will have a better chance of being healthier. The MRI is a two-rule system that can handle multiple funds; in this chapter's example, we start with a family of three funds and:

1. Once a month rank each fund by return that month, then
2. Sell the bottom 25 percent of the portfolio and use the proceeds to buy the top fund.

We have looked at the strengths and weaknesses of each component used in MRI as well as strengths and weaknesses of using MRI; we have compared this to the strengths and weaknesses of conventional pie chart investing.

DEALING WITH STOCK TIPS

E veryone wants to buy the next Microsoft, which is, of course, the software company created by Bill Gates. If you had invested $10,000 in Microsoft back in 1986 when the IPO first came out and just held it, never putting another dime into the stock, your return would have been in the neighborhood of 35,000 percent over an 18-year period. But in 1986 who knew to buy Microsoft? People look at that return and wish they could go back in time and buy Microsoft. And that is the allure of stock tip investing. Everyone is looking to buy the next Microsoft.

Stock tips can come from anywhere. They can come from your long-lost rich uncle, the investor or a high-powered CEO talking on TV. You can pick up a stock tip rumor from your church supper or from a financial newsletter. Stock tips often come with a good story. They are shiny, new, attractive, and seductive, with the promise of a sure way to make lots of money. They are the market's equivalent of a lottery ticket. We all have a tendency to want to invest in something that everyone else is invested in, and we all want others to invest in what we've put our money into. There is a crowd mentality to the hype of stock tips that is enticing to all of us. The danger is that once people invest in a stock on the basis of a tip, they don't want to get out, because they believe it will keep going up and up and they don't want to miss out on making more money with it. Even if the stock goes down, people don't want to sell for fear of missing out, or they hang on just to get even if they can. By far, most stocks do not do as well as hoped. And if you look at this past decade, even moon shots like Microsoft eventually flatten, if not crash.

Funds are safer investments than stocks because, by their nature, they are diversified and thus not as susceptible to idiosyncratic risk. Even if one stock within the fund crashes, it's not going to harm your account too much and you have the added safety net of one of the exit strategies we discussed in previous chapters. Buying any one stock requires more refined ways to deal with idiosyncratic risk, so let's create one. If you are investing in just one stock, the first rule is don't lose more than 1 percent of your portfolio from any one stock. This rule alone means you can have 25 losers in a row and still have an account that is big enough to make a difference (remember, a 25 percent loss requires a 33 percent gain to break even—tough to do but not impossible). The second rule is to use a concept called a trailing stop loss. In order to understand a trailing stop loss, you first need to grasp what a stop-loss order is.

A stop-loss order is an order placed with a broker to sell a stock when it falls to a certain price. It is designed to stop an investor's loss on a position in a stock. If you buy a stock at $10 a share and you put a stop-loss order in at $5/share, if the stock goes down to $5 or below, it will automatically trigger a sell order and you will get out of that stock. A *trailing* stop loss is a more fluid tool since it automatically ratchets up the stop trigger as the stock reaches new high prices from when you bought. Here's how a trailing stop loss works: If you have stock at $10 a share, and you decide you want to sell the stock if the price drops more than 25 percent, the initial trailing stop loss is set at $7.50. As soon as your stock falls to $7.50 per share, a sell order will be triggered. But if the stock goes up to $11 a share, the trailing stop loss will automatically go up to $8.25. (Your broker will automatically ratchet up the stop loss every time your stock reaches a higher price.) If the stock goes up to $12 a share, the trailing-stop-loss order automatically goes up to $9 a share.

So now let's combine the two rules of never losing more than 1 percent on any one stock and using a 25 percent trailing-stop-loss order. If you have an account worth $100,000, the most you want to lose on any one stock would be 1 percent of that account, which would be $1,000. If you bought the $10 stock and you don't want to lose more than $1,000 when the stock drops by 25 percent, you can buy $4,000 worth of that stock. So if the stock goes down to $7.50 a share, you're out with only a $1,000 loss and can live to invest another day. Your hot stock tip ended up being a dud, and that's all the damage it did because you followed this rule. But if the stock goes up to $11 a share, the trailing stop loss goes up to $8.25. If the stock goes up to $12 a share, the stop goes up to $9. And when the stock goes up to $13.33 a share, this is where the magic happens. The trailing stop loss is now at $10 a share. Essentially, there is no more risk unless the stock gaps down below $10, but that is a rare event. Once your stop loss is at your cost point, you can go ahead and buy another $4,000 worth of the stock and again risk only $1,000. And as the stock moves up another 33 percent to $17.77 a share, your risk is again, essentially, zero and you can buy another $4,000 worth of stock. The trailing stop loss is one way to scale into a purchase made on a stock tip without risking more than 1 percent of your portfolio.

If the stock drops below 25 percent and you did not have the trailing-stop-loss order in place, you're pretty much stuck with waiting for the stock to go back up if you refuse to sell. But remember it has to come back up not 25 percent but rather 33 percent just to *break even*. And the lower it drops, the more you've lost. "But wait," comes the popular reply, "the loss isn't 'real' unless I sell!" I wish I had a nickel for every time I heard that phrase. Those words are the sound of a dying account.

One thing to be aware of with this system is that it's hard for a young investor without significant funds to make this work. Let's say you only have a $1,000 account. If you can only invest 4 percent of your portfolio in any one stock, you can only invest $40 in a stock. Unless a stock is less than $40, it's doubtful you'd be able to buy even one share. And if you could get shares, the commissions themselves are, typically, $8–10 per trade, so you'd have to make 25 percent on that stock just to make up for the commissions.

I want to share an example of how some radiologist colleagues and I played a stock representing an amazing technology that promised to revolutionize one of our imaging modalities. Several of my colleagues saw the potential of this technology and based on the demo alone, without looking at the company financials, without looking at its track record, and without looking at anything else except the machine and its story, started to pile into the stock. Some were lucky enough to get into it back in 2004 when the stock was around $20–$30 a share.

HOW I BOUGHT ON A STOCK TIP EXAMPLE

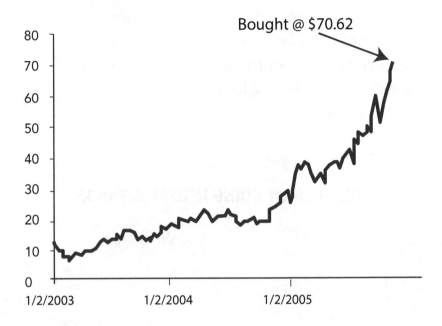

Figure 7.1. In 2004 this new imaging technology had much promise. Colleagues had already bought when the price was around $30–$40 a year before, and when I heard them talking excitedly about it as the price shot up in 2005, I bought in at $70.62.

The stock went up, and I caught wind of it toward the end of 2005. I told my colleagues, "Sure, I'll buy into it, but I'll only use a small position." At that time, I was using a strict exit strategy based on a 50-day moving average.

At that time, I used different criteria for stop loss, but the concept was the same: a stop loss that ratcheted up as the price of the stock made new highs. I had observed the stock's pattern on the chart, and by simply looking at the chart, I saw that the momentum was still up. My colleagues thought the stock had already gone up so much by this time that they were surprised I had bought in. Yet, at the same time, they did not sell what they had because they were sure the stock would keep going up. Notice how the mind can hold contradictory beliefs when real money is involved and the limbic system is engaged. My colleagues had no exit strategy, but I told them I would stay in the stock until it hit my stop loss at the 50-day moving average. They asked me to notify them when I was out. After the stock climbed a bit more, it dropped to my stop loss within a few months, and I was out.

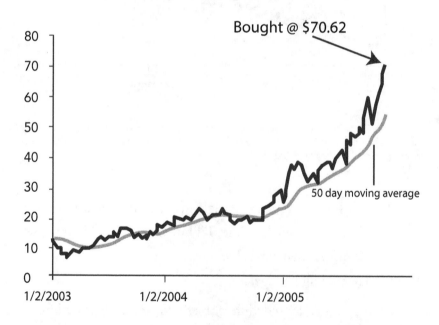

Figure 7.2. I observed that the stock was respecting its 50-day moving average, here plotted graphically for reference. As long as the stock remained above the grey 50-day moving average line, it was safe to stay in it. If, however, the stock crashed below...

HOW I GOT OUT

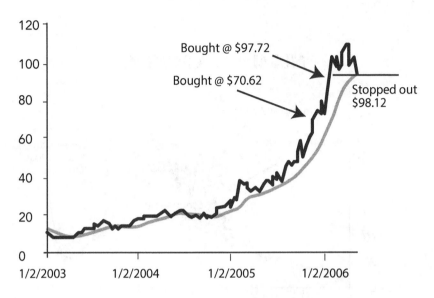

Figure 7.3. As the stock rose, I bought more at $97.72. When the stock started losing steam and began to fall, it crossed the 50-day moving average, and I sold at a profit of $98.12 per share. My colleagues, who asked me to inform them when I sold, chose to hold on.

When I informed my colleagues of this and suggested they get out as well, they rejected my advice because they believed the stock would continue to climb. You can pretty much guess the rest of the story. I got out. They stayed in.

The numbers looked like this: I bought in when the stock was at $70.62 a share. Shortly after that, it split, so each stock I had was now worth two, and I bought more shares at $48.86 a share (presplit equivalent of $97.72 a share). Less than six months later, the stock hit the trailing-stop-loss order I had set and I got out with a gain of almost 20 percent. I made a few thousand dollars on that stock because my position was small compared to the hundreds of thousands of dollars my colleagues had put in. They ultimately lost their money because the stock crashed before they got out, and it hasn't recovered since.

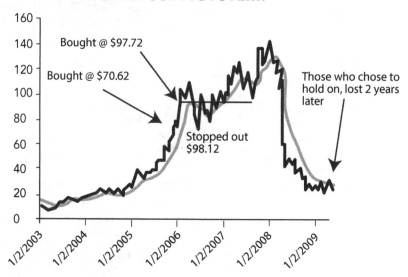

MORAL: USE A SYSTEM!

Figure 7.4. After I got stopped out, the stock price, while still managing to rise, was choppier before it started crashing less than two years later. Those who stayed in lost half their money as their $40 stock purchases saw values of $20.

What kept them in when I got out? When I first got in, I told my colleagues that I'd get out at point X. And they told me, "Great, tell us when you get to that point so we can get out too." But when the time actually came, they didn't. They stayed in, not because they didn't respect my opinion but because of fear and greed. They were afraid of losing out on more gains, and they still believed they could make more money on that stock. After all, the stock price had only recently been even higher, so there was hope that the stock could return to the higher price and go even higher than that. Add to that the fact they had bought into the "story." The emotional power of their conviction overrode the information the chart was giving them.

The truth is most stock tips don't pan out. First of all, for most tips, by the time they reach the retail investor (you and me), the action on them has already happened. Second, the stories that float around in the rumor universe about a stock aren't always true. And even if there is a small grain of truth to the story, it may not move markets as much as we think it will. By the time the retail investor hears a rumor that a certain stock's value is going to blast through the roof, most of the people who move the market have already moved the market for that stock. A stock's story starts with insiders. When they make trades, they have to file papers with the Securities Exchange Commission (SEC). Larger players such as institutional investors or hedge fund managers have access to the story long before you and I do, because their life's mission is to acquire the newly released information more quickly than we can and thus place the trades for themselves before we can. So when they buy the stock, they are actually buying it much earlier than the rest of us, and they are driving the price up as they do so. By the time we hear the story and look at buying the stock, they've already made their money and are looking to sell. We are quite simply late to the game by the virtue of who we are as players. As physicians, we may be pillars of our communities, but when it comes to retail investing, we are still peons with no special information privileges.

The other thing to keep in mind when evaluating a stock tip is that the hype about a stock isn't necessarily based on its balance sheet. The hype could be about anything. It could be about pending lawsuits. It could be about developments in the pipeline. It could be news about overseas wars or correlated prices in commodities. But it's rarely about any key indicators of how well the stock is doing in its industry. People who bought Enron before it crashed were looking at the hype about its rising earnings and did not realize that, at the same time, its operational cash flow was failing.

So how *do* you find the "true" story of a stock before you buy it? That is an art in and of itself. There are market analysts who spend years trying to find good stocks, and even then, their track records are hit and miss. Even if you have sound fundamentals, you also have the vagaries of the market's background noise. The other factor to keep in mind is that when people buy a stock, they think they are buying a sure thing. They are convinced it will go up, or they wouldn't have bought it. This conviction is based on the theory of intermittent reinforcement. Even though most stock tips don't pan out, every now and then some do, and they do so in such a flashy way—as Microsoft did—it makes you forget about all the stock tips that never panned out. It is the same intermittent reinforcement that addicts gamblers to one-armed bandits in casinos: sometimes, when they pull the lever, they win, even if they never win enough to cover their losses. In effect, every time you follow a stock tip, you play the lottery, and everyone thinks his or her tip is the winning ticket. People don't buy stocks because they think they're going to fail. They buy because they are convinced they are going to win. The irony is that when you buy a lottery ticket, at least you know you're buying a lottery ticket.

One problem with buying a stock as if it were a lottery ticket is that you can spend your entire account on that one stock, hoping for a home run. The good thing about applying the two rules of stock picking that we discussed is that they will keep your losses small, and you'll have reserved cash in case a potential lottery ticket comes along in the form of another stock tip. If you keep your losses small, you'll still be able to invest in new opportunities as they come along, whereas people who invest their whole account in a stock have little capital left after one or two losers. Once you start losing, it's very hard to even break even again.

Here's another example. I picked up a stock tip from a newsletter. We'll call the stock XYZ. In August 2006 I bought XYZ for $37.49 a share (see figure 7.5).

HOW I HANDLED NEWSLETTER STOCK TIP XYZ

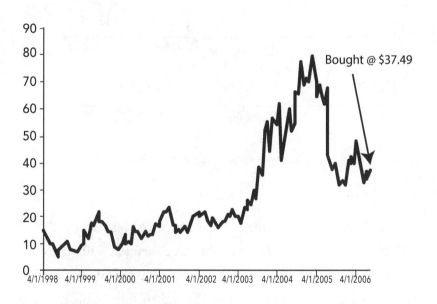

Figure 7.5. I bought XYZ stock from a newsletter tip.

Upon buying XYZ, I immediately placed a 25 percent trailing-stop-loss order so that if the stock were to go down to 75 percent of its price (x $37.49 = $28.12), it would automatically sell. However, if the stock were to go up, the stop price would also ratchet up. I also kept in mind how much a 33 percent gain would be (33 percent gain on $37.49 = $49.97; see figure 7.6).

WHAT I WAS VISUALIZING WHEN BUYING STOCK XYZ

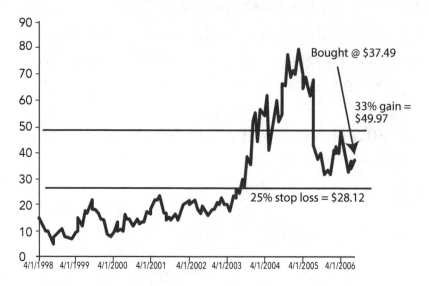

Figure 7.6. This graph shows the purchase of XYZ, with the 25 percent stop-loss line and the 33 percent profit line.

In February 2007, when the stock price went above $49.97 ($37.49 x 1.333 = $49.97), I bought more shares at $50.20 a share. In June 2007, when the stock was above $66.92 ($50.20 x 1.333 = $66.92), I bought in again at $67.17, and in July I bought shares again at $89.31 a share ($67.17 x 1.333 = $89.54). (The stock went above $89.54 but dipped below as I got in). By the end of July, the stock hit a high of $91.79 and started dropping until, on August 16, I sold all my shares at $68.86/share, 25 percent off the high. The stock's price had hit my trailing-stop-loss order (see figure 7.7).

HOW I EVENTUALLY HANDLED STOCK XYZ

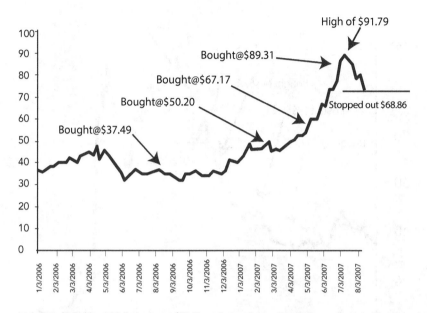

Figure 7.7. After initially buying at $37.49, each time the stock gained approximately 33 percent, I bought more at $50.20, $67.17, and $89.31. After the stock made a high of $91.79, it could not go up a penny more and started falling. Twenty-five percent down from $91.79 is $68.86, which is when the automatic trailing stop loss triggered.

Overall, I made almost 26% on that stock in a little more than one year, while only risking 1 percent of my account. "Well, wait a minute," an astute observer would ask, "if you went in whole hog, initially, at $37.49, you would've made a lot more when you got stopped out at $68.86." True. And going in whole hog (using 100 percent of the portfolio versus only 4 percent of the portfolio) would have risked 25 percent of the portfolio instead of only 1 percent of the portfolio if the stock dropped. Remember when we first buy, no matter how good the story, we don't know how the stock will actually perform. No one has a crystal ball.

WHAT ULTIMATELY HAPPENED TO THE STOCK XYZ

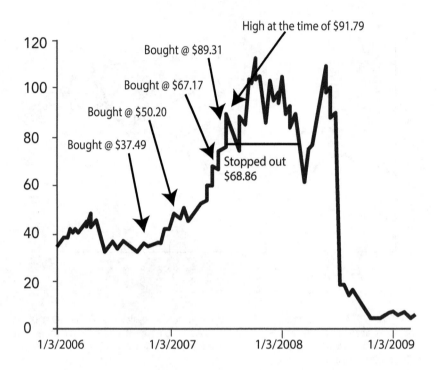

Figure 7.8. Can we get whipsawed with a stop (stock goes higher after we sell)? Of course, we can. But in this case, had we held on with no exit strategy, the stock would have crashed two years later, and we would have lost 90 percent of our investment.

Obviously, if I had sold one month earlier, I would have made more money, but then again, one month earlier, the stock was still trending up. Once the stock started losing more than 25 percent, I avoided the many more losses that came when the stock crashed (see figure 7.8 above). If you are going to play stocks, you have to put your rules in place and follow them. Once the trades are done, you have to be happy with the profits that you made or be happy your small loss didn't become a bigger loss and not lament what might have been had you been gifted with 20/20 hindsight. When a stock falls by 25 percent, it is no longer a stable stock. Instead of thinking, "I could have gotten out higher," you need to tell yourself, "I'm so glad I got out just as it started to destabilize."

A general note about stories and how they affect our investing: as human beings, we like to think of ourselves as rational creatures, especially after going through the rigorous, science-based training of medical school and residency. We are, however, wired to understand the world through stories and the meanings we attach to stories. When something bad happens to us, we may ask ourselves, "Why is God punishing me?" or we may view the experience as a challenge, or we may become angry. These are just three of many emotional responses we may have to an experience. Nowhere is this more evident than in the stock market. You buy a stock for $10. It goes up to $15 and you sell. A profit! You're a genius! Then you see, the next day, that the stock went up to $20. How do you feel now? Most would regret having sold. Or let's say the stock you bought for $10 went down to $5. You sell. A loss, bummer! Yet the next day you see the stock fall even more to $2. Lucky you sold! You're brilliant! But here's the thing: in one case, you made money but felt stupid; in the other case, you lost money but felt like a genius. Stories mess with your head, cause stress, and burn you out. If you decide on your exit strategy before you even go into a stock position, before your stories start to cause doubt and turmoil, your stomach will thank you for keeping the ulcers away.

There are many factors that can move the market, and there are many ways to trade the market. Warren Buffet is the iconic example of a pure fundamental investor. He looks solely at the financial numbers. He knows how to read the financial statements and how to weed out the ticking time bombs. And he knows when the numbers are good. Furthermore, he actually knows the people who make the decisions at the company he's looking to invest in. His number-one rule of investing? Don't lose money. Yet he claims his exit strategy is to hold forever. But the truth is stocks do lose money, eventually, and even Buffett has been known to sell. The difference is someone like Buffett can afford a lot more of a loss than can you and I. And someone like Buffett can also go to the company's board of directors and say, "This is what's wrong with the company. Change this." What we need to know about ourselves when investing in a stock is how much of a loss we can realistically handle before we admit that we've made a mistake.

TAKEAWAYS:

Stock tips can be hit or miss, but a 25 percent trailing stop loss on a position that never risks more than 1 percent of your portfolio on any one stock gives you room to be wrong most of the time while still benefiting from the chance you'll pick the next moon-shot stock. Individual stocks can present particularly seductive stories when it comes to investing, thus emotions can blind you to the real dangers of the idiosyncratic risks of individual stocks if you don't religiously follow a set of rules to keep your portfolio out of serious trouble. These rules help you see "how do I know if I'm wrong" when your emotions blind you to objective evidence.

THE PSYCHOLOGY OF INVESTING

You now have enough information to start investing. But some of you still won't invest. Even though they know the rules of an investment system, many investors will never start. Of those who do, many will either change the rules or do the reverse of what the rules tell them to do. Why? It isn't because they aren't smart enough to follow the system. It's because, time after time, psychology will supersede technology. Despite all the data showing that a strategy works, many investors may not trust the system. There is also a certain amount of inertia that comes with doing something new. People tend to not want to do something new in favor of doing something familiar, which in this case is to either do nothing or to continue investing the way they always have: without a plan. And then, there are the death-wish, daredevil fearless but fickle cowboys who will try anything but not for long enough to let it work.

Another reason people don't invest using one of these systems is the belief in a paradigm called passive investing. Passive investing is like passive sex or passive health. You buy, hold, sit still, and pray, hoping to get better or get lucky. As physicians, we all have patients who are noncompliant, who don't take responsibility for their health, or they may blindly follow our suggestions and prescriptions without much insight into what's going on with their health. Those patients will all have different outcomes than what we intend for them. This kind of hands-off approach puts us out of touch with what we're trying to achieve, whether it be health care or investing. Let's face it. No one will watch your portfolio as closely as you will, no matter how much you pay for the service. In life, there are three areas that are virtually impossible to outsource completely: your health, your children, and your finances. Yes, you can hire consultants, coaches, nannies, and doctors, but ultimately, the responsibility in these three areas belongs to you.

So you definitely need to know yourself before you start investing. The passive personality might not ever invest because of fear: fear of getting into the market just when stocks go down or fear of taking any loss at all. Those with aggressive personalities will implement the rules but then change them in the middle of the investment. Instead of using a rules-based method to modify or exit, they may be swayed by media, by rumors, or by gut feelings, or they may project their own interpretation on the charts, countermanding what the rules tell them to do.

For instance, back in 1999, when I was still heavily relying on options, I showed a colleague how to use a two-rule option strategy. The entrance and exit points were very clear-cut. I would sit right next to her, and we would review the chart at the end of the week and go over the rules. I would ask, "Okay, when this stock hits this point and these conditions are met, what are we supposed to do?" The correct answer, according to the rules, was to sell and exit. Despite the fact that my colleague was a prestigious, data-driven person who published research with huge, complex Excel spreadsheets full of statistics that she routinely analyzed, when she looked at this stock data, she gleefully answered, "Buy more!" Why? Her explanation was, "The stock was a good buy at the higher price. The price went down so that means it's a good idea to buy more." But rules exist for a reason. They let us know when there's a high chance that our instincts could be wrong. And if we could be wrong, we need to get out. The concept is to try and minimize our losses because losses are larger than we think; large losses can destroy our portfolio and make it unrecoverable. The smaller the loss, the easier it is to recover and keep investing.

So my colleague and I were sitting there in front of the charts, looking at the same data, and I saw "sell" and she saw "buy." The data showed that when the stock price dropped below a certain number, it was past the point of break even, so it was better to get out with a small loss. But what she saw was a falling stock price, which indicated, in her mind, that she should buy more. Why wasn't she right? Well, she was right that the stock was cheaper. But it was going down, and it was going to continue to go down. How could I know that? Think of the movement of the stocks as a figurative bell curve (see figure 8.1).

If you consider the probability of prices moving up or down as a bell curve, the stock has, approximately, the same chance of going up as going down. Sure, our research (or "reliable stock tip" rumor source) may lead us to believe there is a larger probability of going toward profit than loss (that is why we buy, after all), but the chances of making a profit are closer to 50-50 than we realize. Think of how many of your stock tips have actually been successful.

STATISTICAL EFFECTS OF STOP LOSSES

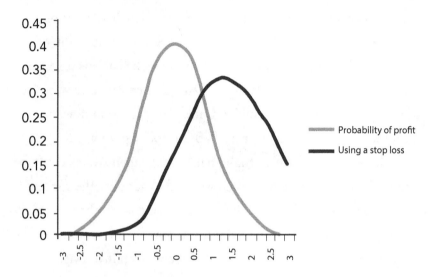

Figure 8.1. The grey bell curve represents, when we buy a stock, the relative probability of making a profit, if there is a 50-50 chance of the stock going up or down. Nuance: The peak of the curve isn't at 0 (breakeven). In fact, the bell curve has already shifted a bit to losses due to commissions and other tangible and intangible costs. When we use a stop loss, for instance, at 1 standard deviation, we've essentially cut off the losing tail below 1 standard deviation and shifted the probability for profit curve to the black line. Nuance: even though we've cut our chances of making larger losses, large losses are still possible, since stocks can still gap down below our stops between trading days.

If we have a stop-loss order, what we're doing is chopping off the bottom tail and shifting the bell curve away from loss. Whereas, if we buy more, we're throwing good money after bad, and we're actually shifting the bell curve toward loss (see figure 8.2).

Curiously, the same bell curve shift toward loss also occurs when investors sell as soon as they make a small profit, justifying the sell with maxims such as "You can't go broke making a profit." Yet they refuse to sell when they start to lose, due to the pain of selling at a loss and the pain of admitting to making a mistake, justifying the hold with adages such as "It isn't a real loss if I just hold on until the stock comes back." It is a real loss whether or not the investor sells.

HOW ADDING TO LOSING POSITIONS WORKS

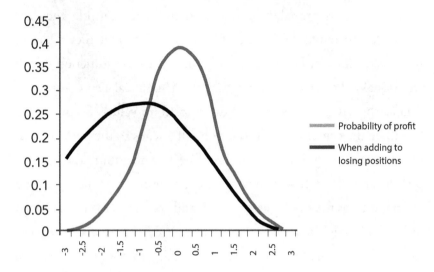

Figure 8.2. A stock's initial potential for profit or loss can be represented by the grey bell curve. If a stock drifts into loss territory, buying more only weighs the outcome more toward loss, shifting the bell curve toward loss (black bell curve).

Part of the psychology of investing is discipline. If the formula requires us to look at the portfolio once a month, that's what we need to do. A challenge with the once-a-month strategy is that some people like to keep monitoring the market many times within the month. They hear doom and gloom news or catch wind of an irrational, exuberant sentiment and run to see how their portfolio is performing. It takes discipline to stick with the original plan. On the other hand, if we ignore or skip months, that's also a lack of discipline. It can hurt us because a once-a-month strategy is designed to lessen our losses and keep them relatively small. If we skip a month and start taking losses that we're not even aware of, those losses can snowball very quickly.

There are emotional needs that are met by deviating from discipline. People who watch the market on a daily basis instead of a monthly basis probably have a need to be in control. They are compelled to reinforce a sense of certainty that what they're doing is correct. Conversely, others may be drawn to the addiction of the emotional roller coaster that comes from financial news stories, as well as the casino-like action of their portfolio values. Some people like to be the center of attention, tying their egos to the performance of a stock, shining in the adulation of peers who admire their stock-picking acumen, refusing to admit the possibility that they could be wrong, even as the stock starts to crash and continues to crash. Others dislike feeling left out when they hear their colleagues discussing the market. They don't like the sense of not being in the know, unaware of what's going on, so they check their portfolio compulsively. Ironically, people who tend to not check, who skip months, also find comfort in the certainty of not doing something. Sticking their heads in the sand and not facing the market, hiding the uncertainties of the market from view is their way of being certain. They deal with their anxiety by not looking. The good news is both of these anxieties, the compulsive desire to keep overloading the brain with daily data and the need to ignore the portfolio, can be assuaged by learning to trust a system that is designed to tackle the big enemy: large market drops.

Granted, trust is hard to build. A system may look good on paper and it may have decades of data supporting it, and yet it can take years to overcome the tendency to think you know better and therefore will make the trade earlier than the system recommends. In my case, when I have overruled my system, almost always, I get crushed. If you fly an airplane, you have to trust your instruments when flying in fog. The minute you decide not to trust your instruments, you're in trouble. It takes real discipline to follow your instruments when every other part of your senses, your being, is telling you something different from what the instruments are telling you. You could be in a death spiral and have only minutes to live and not realize it if it were not for your instruments. Pilots are taught two different ways of flying: one is visual flight reference (VFR) and the other is instrument flight reference (IFR). Most amateurs can do VFR; they can fly in fair weather, they can see the terrain, and they can see the altitude. But the ability to fly the plane relying solely on instruments, especially at night or in foul weather, is crucial for survival. It's easy to underestimate how much discipline that takes because we all want to trust our eyes or our senses. The stock market is essentially counterintuitive too, and so when we use our intuition, which may serve us well in other areas of our lives, it will not serve us well in the market when all the other investors are also trying to do the same thing with their intuition.

Another reason that people either don't start using a system, or once they do start, they don't check it monthly, is that a certain amount of inertia exists in everyone. Taking action, particularly if it's unfamiliar, requires some energy. You have to remember the system, but once it becomes habit, you will start looking forward to the end of the month to see what adjustments you need to make, if any. Once monthly checking becomes a habit, it is exciting to see the progress of your investing. In the same way that the overweight patient who steps on the bathroom scale regularly tends to lose more weight than one who doesn't, success tends to encourage the habits that cause the success.

Some people like to paper trade (simulated trading). They set up an account on paper and when it's time to make a trade, they make it on paper just to see what the mechanics are like. Paper trading is highly recommended as a means of getting acquainted with a system.

However, even after they paper trade successfully, once new investors start using real money, they tend to deviate from the plan.

It took me a while to believe that money has a strong emotional hold on us. Let's go back to the party trick we talked about at the start of this book when we asked friends to take out a $20 bill and rip it in half. Most people can't make themselves do it. There's an absolutely visceral pain associated with tearing a bill. We know this $20 bill, or $100 bill, is just a piece of paper. If we tape it up again, the bank will accept it. It doesn't lose any value, and yet, we can't bring ourselves to do it. We venerate paper money on a deep emotional level.

As doctors, we are trained to order tests, and once we order them, we're obligated to respect the results of the tests. So one reason that physicians shoot themselves in the foot by watching the market too closely every day is that they are used to getting lots of data they somehow feel obligated to act on. A strategy that advocates only making decisions on data that comes out once a month, making all other data irrelevant, goes against the grain for them. If you're trained to respect the results of the tests you ordered, but you don't follow through on them, it just feels wrong. When I was in medical school, one of my attending physicians stressed the importance of only ordering labs when there was a clinical need. For instance, if we take a daily lab, and one day the white blood cell count spikes, are we necessarily going to do anything different for the patient, based on this one lab value? No, we'll probably just repeat the labs to see if it was a fluke. Another example is that, with the rise of CT scans, we're finding all these incidental lesions. And because we find these lesions, we feel obligated to completely work up each lesion with more invasive tests that have their own morbidity and mortality risks. It used to be assumed that if you found a lung nodule, you were obliged to biopsy it, even though, ten years ago, the survival rate for even a small, early-stage malignancy was not great. Frequently, patients who didn't have lung cancer would suffer severe consequences, including death, from biopsies that had complications. I call it the tyranny of too much data. We now have algorithms to deal with data from diseases such as lung nodules, but controversy still exists because technology continues to advance faster than our data can support it. And this is the same concept in the market.

If we take in too much data, and we feel we have an obligation to do something with it, our natural tendency is to override our system in favor of taking action. We can address this particular gnawing sense of anxiety by realizing that monitoring our portfolio once a month is sufficient to catch major trends relatively early. More frequent adjustments, like the complications of a biopsy, could kill a portfolio. Conversely, the danger of checking only every three months, or waiting too long, is that you will miss something. If breast cancer cells have 40-day to 325-day doubling times, even a cancer with a particularly aggressive 20-day doubling time would take two years from inception to become detectable on mammogram. Hence, annual screenings would help detect cancers at earlier stages. Try not to skip them. Whipsaws and other trading costs are the equivalent of the costs of negative biopsies. We'd rather work up a false positive than miss a true cancer or market crash. If you wait too long to check, the incipient bear market could wipe out a large amount of your portfolio before you catch it with your system. And it takes longer to recover from a larger loss. The whole point of following a system is to deal with those losses while they are *still small*.

Arrogance is another emotional barrier. The successful investors I know well tend to be humble because they've gone through several episodes of having their accounts blow up. My goal is to try to encourage and teach successful investing so others won't have to go through as many painful episodes of loss in their lives. We can shortcut the path to wisdom by learning from our predecessors. Just as the best investors make mistakes, the best doctors can misdiagnose or prescribe a treatment that has a bad outcome. Over time, inevitably, we make mistakes. We learn from our own experiences and the experiences of others. The dangerous thing about arrogance is that we don't know we ourselves are arrogant until we get a wake-up call. Arrogance is created by success without reflection. If you invest, you will be successful, over time, but you will also make mistakes. That's okay, as long as you learn from those mistakes. You don't want to be so blind that you keep repeating the same errors with your portfolio any more than you want to keep using the wrong procedure on your patients.

In my case, back in 2003–2004, I had had 17 straight months of wins with my options trading. I knew that trading options was a risky business. Therefore, I had a system, a moderately complex system with several rules to help me protect myself against large losses. After more than a year of winning, I became complacent and arrogant enough to start disregarding the rules in my own system. I disregarded six of my own rules, and when the market went against me, I was wiped out. Arrogance, ironically, can coexist with fear, but in my case, it wasn't arrogance masking fear, it was arrogance from too much success.

To make another comparison to the health field, in radiology we look at routine X-rays. Sometimes we look at an X-ray and there's a major finding, a fracture for instance. We become so happy about that finding that we miss the second fracture, or we miss a more subtle bone tumor elsewhere. The lesson I learned, as a radiologist, is that every time we miss and get feedback, we keep our arrogance in check and become more humble. Subsequently, each time we look at another scan, we trust our search patterns more than our gestalt. This applies to the market system as well. If you're knowledgeable and you're confident with your system, you're going to do well. But if you become arrogant, you're going to miss something. And the distinction between being confident and arrogant is this: if you're confident, you trust your system, whether it's your system of looking at scans or your system of investing. If you're arrogant, you disregard your systems, thinking you know better.

New investors who look at too much market data or are inexperienced with a system might feel overwhelmed and think, "Yikes, I have to look at all these different numbers and make all these calculations. What if I'm wrong?" Or they might not know where to find the data to make the necessary calculations or be able to determine which data are important and which are useless. They're confused and anxious. It's kind of like medical school where we are drinking from a fire hose of information during our years of training and trying to make sense of it all. The good news with the market is that we can spend a lifetime analyzing why the market does what it does, just as we can spend a lifetime understanding human physiology and pathophysiology. But in the end, most treatments are ultimately straightforward if they're evidence based. Similarly, the investment systems of a market are pretty straightforward once we establish clarity on what information is important at what times. How do we get this clarity? One of my professors, who lectured on how to read EKGs, told us, "The best way to learn how to read EKGs is to read EKGs." I can list all the rules of investing in this book, but unless we actually implement the system, we'll never be able to transfer the knowledge from our heads to our physiology, to the act of doing. Making mistakes is part of the learning curve. But at least, the faster we learn to use the system, the less chance of an investment wipeout.

To go back to the EKG example, as medical students, we did not just read live patients' EKGs off the bat. There are ways to receive feedback on your skills before going live. As far as concerns the stock market, the good news is there is no shortage of old chart data and historical prices on which to practice. There is also no rule that you must commit live money to the market at the start; you can always "paper trade," making hypothetical trades on paper as if you had a live account, while you get used to the system and get a feel for routinely implementing your system.

Another psychological barrier to success is the subconscious belief in limits. There is a number, whether we are conscious of it or not, that controls how much we make and keep. Consider how people tend to die on Monday mornings or around major holidays or other life milestones such as significant birthdays. We believe we will live to a certain age and hang on just long enough to reach that milestone. Financially, we also have internal thermostats limiting how much we believe we should earn or how much we should be worth. Companies' attempts at growing sales by increasing their salesmen's commissions paradoxically decreased sales, since the salesmen figured they needed to sell less to reach their level of comfortable or accustomed income. Lottery winners tend to end up more broke or in debt than they were before they won the lottery. Traders tend to consistently grow their accounts to a certain size before blowing them up, all from a likely subconscious belief about how much they think they should be worth. Until that identity changes, their limits will persist.

We have talked about confusion being an emotional barrier to successful investing, but we can learn to use it to our advantage. If we're confused about what to do next, we have the resources to help us out of our fog. Those resources include education through reading, seminars, and discussions with peers or consultants. There are other types of confusion as well. For instance, once you are in the market but are not clear about your plan, you begin to second-guess yourself, "Gee, should I sell? Should I not sell?" That type of confusion can range anywhere from a low but gnawing sense of anxiety to outright panic, and it is deadly because it means either you don't have a plan or your plan is incomplete. Once confusion turns into outright emotion, such as fear and greed, you become a pig or sheep that is slaughtered in the market. The saying on Wall Street is that bulls and bears will win eventually, but pigs and sheep get slaughtered. Think back to your intern year when you had to conduct a code. You memorized the advanced cardiovascular life support (ACLS) protocols and algorithms, but in the moment of the event you felt time pressure. A real live human being—or practice dummy with an instructor watching and judging you—was in front of you. Unless you can control that panic, you won't remember the system. Maintaining calm, trusting that you know the system, remembering the system, and utilizing the system go a long way toward breaking the barrier of confusion.

In order to become successful investors, we need to break these emotional barriers to money. We can reduce our fear if we know that a system is built primarily to decrease the chances of loss. That allows us to sleep better at night. Greed and fear are similar because part of greed is the fear of losing out on huge gains. That's why we tend to invest in stocks or in mutual funds that performed extremely well the previous year. Because our emotional barrier blinds us to reality, we think that if a stock or mutual fund has a history of doing well, it will keep doing well. Part of the solution to that illusion is to realize that major trends tend to last about 9 to 16 months. Last year's stock or mutual fund winners have a look-back period of 12 months, which means it is extremely likely that we are late in catching the uptrend, if we have not already missed the uptrend completely.

If we accept the premise that our emotional perceptions of money are no more than interpretations of fact, we can change them. Everything that happens in life is a fact, but we interpret those facts through our own stories. When something bad happens to us, some of us react by feeling sorry for ourselves ("Oh, my God, I just knew it, why does this always happen to me?"). Others ask more growth-oriented questions, ("What can we learn from this?" or "where is the gift in this?"). Yet others use the experience to empower themselves ("Challenge accepted. Bring it on."). The language we use affects the meaning we give ourselves and ultimately affects our emotional state and vice versa. If someone came up to you and said, "I think you're mistaken" versus "You're wrong" versus "You're lying"—would you have different biochemical reactions to those different choices of words? We do not often chose our words consciously. And so it is with money. The most common stories we tell ourselves about money are that we never have enough money or that we are no good with money. If these messages are repeated often enough, they become a self-fulfilling prophecy.

One way to become more self-aware of our attitude to money is a simple exercise that we can perform in ten minutes, preferably with a partner to keep us honest. Ask yourself to finish the statement, "money is _____." Don't think about it. Don't pause. Just keep writing down everything that comes into your mind. If you're the accountability partner for the exercise, keep prodding your partner to continue writing if he or she pauses. Then, repeat the exercise with these other statements:

Money is NOT _____

Not having money is_____

Having money is_____

Wealth is_____

Being rich is _____

I want money for _____

I am already rich because _____

I am _____ of money

Rich people are_____

Poor people are _____

Keep writing the thoughts that fill in those blanks for you. After ten minutes of doing this, you'll find contradictory words and phrases popping up. These give a clue to the nature of some of our subconscious conflicts. Insight is the first part of learning how to understand and deal with ourselves. Once we detect these potential conflicts, we have a great place to start growing.

When something unexpectedly horrible happens, we mutter expletives and negative phrases that direct our subconscious to look at the world negatively. But expressing a simple alternative, such as "Hoorah!", each time something unexpected happens encourages us to look at the positive side of things, the possibilities of what we can do. In investing, when we lose money, we think, "Gee, I'm an idiot." When we make money, we think, "Gee, I'm a genius." What is more effective is to ask ourselves whether we followed the rules of the system. If we made money but didn't follow the rules, that's failure. However, if we lost money but did follow the rules, that's still success.

Years ago when I was an intern and had my first paycheck, I thought all I needed to do was be frugal and make sure my bills were paid, but in reality, that was not enough. I needed to address the fact that many decisions are emotionally driven. I grew up as a typical kid who watched a lot of TV and movies. I was, like most kids, inundated with messages that villains were rich and power-hungry guys, wealthy people were evil, and greedy people were evil—all themes that make for a good story. But such messages forced me to discount or reject parts of myself that are common to everyone. We all need a certain amount of greed and a sense of self-preservation and self-interest to survive and grow in this environment. Becoming a doormat serves no one. To create a healthy balance of the "negative" and "positive" is more important to our growth than to vilify any one aspect of ourselves. Overcoming these emotional barriers helps us become more balanced in self-awareness and better integrated in society.

TAKEAWAYS:

Money plays a role in life, just like anything else. It's a component of life on a deep, emotional level. We need to recognize, accept, and channel the emotions that influence how we deal with our finances. To change our financial destiny, we need to change our emotional interpretations of money, both on a conscious and subconscious level. Any attempt at investing, or taking any other positive action, will be doomed to failure if our emotions are in conflict or we struggle with identity challenges, whether we are aware of such conflicts or not.

COMMON QUESTIONS AND ANSWERS

Now that I've shared my background with you, the philosophy behind my investing strategies, the different systems themselves, and the emotional factors that determine how well we use them, I will share with you some questions I'm frequently asked and my answers, which may be of interest to you too.

Effective investing systems are a dime a dozen. The four systems I have outlined in this book have worked consistently for me, as long as I use them with discipline. With them, I've managed to create another income stream for myself, one that involves no employees and no lawsuits. It took me less than 20 years to achieve. The financial part of our lives is often neglected or misunderstood. A well-rounded life includes mastery in this area as well.

Q: I'm a busy physician. I don't have time to do this myself. Is it worth it for me to pay somebody?

A: If you want to pay someone to do this for you, you can. But when you look for someone, be sure to find out if the money manager is a broker or a fiduciary.

Q: What's the difference between a broker and a fiduciary?

A: A fiduciary, by law, works for you in your best interest. If you were to find out the fiduciary did not work in your best interest and, for instance, sold you high-fee funds that benefited the fiduciary more than you, you can sue. Brokers only have to meet the suitability standard, which means that as long as whatever they're selling you is "suitable," they can sell you anything that sounds reasonable. The standards governing brokers are much lower. An analogy that people like to make contrasts nutritionists with butchers: If you're hungry for steak and you go to a nutritionist, that specialist will advise you on the basis of your dietary needs. If you're hungry for steak, and you go to a butcher, that specialist will ask you which cut you want. A broker is a butcher; you'll just get what you ask for in their inventory. A fiduciary will look at the larger financial picture.

Q: Are there any questions I should ask a money manager?

A: It is important to ask about and understand the manager's risk management system.

Q: Why should I ask about my money manager's risk management system?

A: Often, a money manager will ask you to fill out a risk assessment profile, which is, basically, a quiz. You will be pigeonholed in a "risk tolerance" category; the allocation of your portfolio will then be placed in some type of pie chart to reflect that level of risk tolerance, with periodic balancing, and likely slight readjustment to the pie chart as you pass through different stages of life. That's management up to a point. As we discussed earlier, you won't lose as much with this type of portfolio as you would with the worst fund or asset class in your pie chart, but you won't make as much as the best fund or asset class would either. Another red flag to watch for is if your manager claims the firm has a large team specializing in the management of your portfolio. What this could mean is that the firm has a large overhead. If you see that the firm has a proprietary and complex stock-picking or dynamic asset allocation strategy, again, you want to understand the system before you invest. The firm may refuse to disclose its methodology on the grounds of proprietary information, even if you ask to sign a nondisclosure agreement (to me, a red flag). If a company were to sell you a black box, how secure would you be with a black box you didn't understand? How would you know when you should have gotten out, but didn't, if you didn't know the black box criteria? What would happen to your portfolio if the black box company were to go bankrupt or disappear? Be sure your money manager can clearly explain the firm's risk management system. Many times money managers cannot explain it to you because they outsource this part of their practice and do not themselves understand it. Another way you can check out the risk management system is to ask what the firm's exit strategy is. No system is foolproof. Every system should have a "what-if-I'm-wrong?" exit strategy.

Q: Any other questions I should ask my money manager?

A: If your money manager presents a model portfolio that includes several funds, ask how those funds compare with no-load index funds. In other words, ask why you should invest with that portfolio when you could just buy an index mutual fund. If your money manager claims that a particular fund or group of funds "are appropriate for their strategy when comparing to particular benchmark index funds," (regulations discourage advisors from using words such as 'beat') you can explore this by researching online. Don't just look at one-year, five-year, or ten-year returns; these figures can be manipulated by many methods. Look at actual historical data that are available through free websites such as finance.yahoo.com. Be sure to look at the dividend-adjusted data. Information is readily available; it truly is the great equalizer. Extremely few actively managed funds consistently beat index funds over time. If your money manager seeks to improve fund performance through tactical real-location of index funds (such as with one of the systems presented in this book), ask for an explanation of the system. When money managers approach me, I often ask if they will teach me their system because if I cannot understand it, I will not invest with them. They will, typically, try to evade that question by claiming their system is too complex to teach, which is another red flag—if there are so many moving parts, isn't the system more likely to incur errors or add to more overhead?

Q: What is the benefit to your money manager of putting you into a fund that does less than what that manager tells you it's going to do?

A: A broker will say that a stock fund exposes you to stocks, which are an asset class that meets the modern portfolio criterion of diversification. The more erudite managers will point to a 1986 paper by Brinson,

Hood, and Beebower (such a famous paper that it is now referred to as the BHB) that "proved" that 93.6 percent of the average fund's return is a result of asset allocation, not necessarily the selection of any one stock or security within that asset class. I analyzed several sample portfolios offered by money managers who seemed genuinely enthusiastic that what they were proposing would work. I needed more than just their word, so I double-checked, using historical data. What they were proposing would work in theory under MPT and BHB. Yet when I analyzed the actual data, the component funds were found to be lagging behind their respective index or benchmark. Back-testing would often reveal that had the funds been tactically reallocated, using a variant of MRI, performance would have improved. When I, as a prospective client, presented this data to those money managers, they did not want to hear. Perhaps, they did not know what they were advocating, or they would not have, in good conscience, suggested those funds or those particular mixes of funds. Of course, there are others who are not fiduciaries who knowingly advocate their own in-house high-fee funds.

Q: Is my money manager being paid by the funds themselves for putting me into them, as well as charging me a fee?

A: Remuneration rates are byzantine. Even after the bear market crash of 2007–2008 when new legislation was introduced to simplify and make remuneration schedules more transparent, they remain complicated. If you were to ask any money managers how much they are paid, or how they get paid, or if you ask your own money manager for a list of fees charged for managing your portfolio, they frequently can't give you an exact figure.

Q: What is the difference between a cumulative average and a mathematical average?

A: When you ask your manager for a cumulative average (sometimes known as "annualized return") of a sample fund or sample portfolio your manager handles or a cumulative average of the model that used to manage your portfolio, the more years' worth of data or back-tested data you are given, the better. If what you get is a regular average, all you're getting is a mathematical average. For instance, a fund that rose by 50 percent one year and fell by 50 percent the next year averaged 0 percent in terms of a mathematical average. But if a cumulative average is used, the fund actually lost 25 percent (100 up 50 percent = 150; 150 down 50 percent = 75; likewise 100 down 50 percent = 50; 50 up 50 percent = 75; the order doesn't matter), so the cumulative, or annualized, average of the two years would be -13.4 percent (on average, each year, the system lost 13.4 percent, losing 25 percent in two years).

If you can, get a graph of the performance of an actual portfolio or a model portfolio, or get a back-tested graph of the proposed portfolio or system. Make sure you know whether you're looking at a linear graph or a log graph. (The curves will appear distorted if you're not used to looking at that type of graph.) You'll get a better understanding of these "return" data, and of how volatile (choppy) the price movement can be. Look particularly at years 2000–2002 and 2007–2009 to see how the portfolio fared during those periods of major bear markets.

Q: Can I ask my money manager to utilize specific risk management strategies, such as rotating the pie chart for me or placing trailing stops for me?

A: If your money manager suggests a pie chart for you, you can always ask to have the pie chart components periodically rotated. This can be done monthly or at the very least, quarterly. In other words, every month or every quarter, the bottom 25 percent of the portfolio would be sold and the top fund bought. Be prepared for a "no" answer and be prepared to act on that answer. If you want your money manager to buy stocks for you based on stock tips, either ones you get or ones your manager recommends, you can ask that a 25 percent trailing stop be placed on these trades and that they be appropriately sized to reduce the impact of losses on your portfolio. Nowadays, you can easily place trailing stops online by yourself, in which case, ask what would be the added value of having a money manager.

Q: What do I do if my money manager says, "That isn't the way we do things. It's unnecessary," and he tells me there's no reason to check my portfolio more than once a year?

A: *It is somewhat ironic that money managers advise not checking too often as well as checking at least once a year. We check portfolios for a reason, in the same way we order tests on patients for a reason. If we order a test or we check the portfolio, we intend to act on the results. We're looking for specific criteria within our plan to adjust to developing market conditions. We already know why we check more than once a year, using the systems outlined in this book: major trends usually last 9 to 16 months. If we check just once a year, and we try to buy last year's winner, we're usually buying last year's winner toward the end of its winning run, which is why buying last year's winner generally doesn't work. But if we do it more often, such as once a quarter or once a month, the chances are greater that we might catch a major uptrend somewhere near its beginning.*

Q: I've never invested before. I understand medicine. I understand science, but I don't understand investments. I don't know how the stock market works. Maybe I should just stay away from it.

A: *Well, congratulations! You went through medical school, which requires a lot of learning with a lot of math. Every time you take a continuing medical education seminar or read a medical journal, you incorporate graphs and charts full of data in your fund of professional knowledge. When you say that you don't understand investing, it just means that you're not familiar with how to start. I know that was the case for me. When I started, I had a money manager who charged high fees. But once I learned how to open up an account and placed my first trade, a psychological barrier was broken. Ignorance imprisons us with fear. Knowledge, augmented by experience, empowers us.*

Q: How do I begin to learn?

A: *Reading the book you are holding in your hands right now is a start. Don't let your pride get in the way of asking for help from someone who has been there before. Friends, family members, or colleagues who already have started investing can give you their perspectives on how they got started. Hiring a money manager who's on your side (i.e., a fiduciary) can also help ease you into the world of investing. Resources are out there. Make the decision to keep an open mind and step up rather than hold on to the fears that keep you imprisoned in a world of ignorance.*

Q: What if I make a mistake?

A: *If you make a mistake, learn and move on. In general, start small so when you do make your first mistake, it won't be big. You can even start with paper trading—whatever it takes to minimize your fear of making* *a mistake. When you become more confident that you understand what it is you're doing, you can incrementally increase your position.*

Mistakes happen. Mistakes are a part of life. We've been taught in school to not make mistakes, when, in actuality, our best learning comes from mistakes. I'm not encouraging you to make mistakes on purpose, although you can always learn something through trial and error by varying variables in your technique (that's called experimentation, performed in controlled environments). But just switch your mentality to one of knowing there are no mistakes, only results. If you don't like the results, change your behavior. The fact that you're reading this book and are willing to learn from others (who most likely made their own fair share of mistakes) means you're willing to learn from the mistakes of others. Congratulations. You're saving yourself years of trial and error.

Q: Are there unique financial problems that physicians face?

A: *Investing is only one challenge that we physicians face. It is a good idea to have a team of advisors, consisting of an estate planning lawyer, an accountant, an overall financial advisor, and maybe, a money manager, to help make sure that your basics are covered. Just as you expect your patients to understand and be actively involved in their own medical and health care, don't completely abdicate those estate and financial responsibilities to the "pros." Again, no one will watch your nest egg and your family more closely than you will.*

One unique challenge that we face as physicians, besides taxes and estate planning issues, is the potential for lawsuits. Even excellent physicians can get sued for bad outcomes that are inevitable in any busy practice. The people you choose to be on your team will help you with this unique challenge. There are some structures, such as retirement plans and permanent insurance, that protect our assets against creditors, and you can review these with your estate attorney.

Q: Are the systems you describe widely used?

A: The dollar cost averaging system has been around for decades. This is a system that every basic money manager uses. Traders use variations of the moving average indicator all the time, albeit, usually, in shorter time frames to capitalize on shorter-term market trends. There are investors and investment newsletter publishers who use a long, 20-month moving average as an indicator to gauge whether or not it's relatively safe to invest in stocks in general or in particular stocks. Sector rotation systems have been around for years. As I mentioned, it was in 1995 that I started reading a newsletter that used a sector rotation system. There are several software programs out there that provide sector rotation for thousands of clients, including money managers. The trailing-stop-loss concept is a common trader tool. The MRI is a monthly rotation system. It doesn't use sectors, so you can't really call it a sector rotation system, but it does rotate asset classes. None of the systems highlighted in this book is a quick, fly-by-night, untested investment system. This doesn't mean there are no risks. Technically, every investment has risks, which is why I've outlined the risks of each system. They're not just back-tested. I have used variations of these systems for the past 19 years, including through the last two big bear markets. It is true that past performance doesn't guarantee future results, but it's also true that if a system doesn't even pass back-testing, it's probably not going to do well in the future either.

Q: What does success look like? How do I know when I'm sufficiently well off?

A: This is a personal question that will be different for everyone, depending on life circumstances. There is a theory that for every bag of gold you earn, if you keep one coin before spending the rest, and keep accumulating that pile of coins, eventually, and sooner than you think, you'll be "golden." In another interpretation of financial security, you would add up all your monthly obligatory bills, such as utilities, mortgage, transportation, food, and insurance, and multiply that yearly total by 25. The number is, usually, surprisingly low. If you had an account of that size and it rose by just 4 percent per year, that income could keep you financially secure for the rest of your life. And the more accurate you can make that picture, the clearer your goal will be and the more empowered you will feel. Obviously, this calculation is simplistic and doesn't add in factors such as projected inflation, projected tax brackets, desires for basic luxuries such as entertainment, clothes, dreams, and so on. But at least, this calculation gives you a ballpark number to strive for, initially. Some people have high lifestyle costs. Other people have low lifestyle costs. Some people are happy driving a Prius. Other people have to drive a Tesla. You have to determine the standard of living you're happiest with or are comfortable with to know when you've reached your financial goal. Keep in mind the Hedonic Treadmill: as incomes rise, expectations and desires also rise, and happiness gained by attaining goals and dreams often does not last as long as we expect. The day you become wealthy is when you break the Hedonic Treadmill and trade expectation for appreciation.

Q: What's the best question you've asked yourself?

A: Our lives are guided by questions, whether we're conscious of them or not. But one question that has served me well, both financially and in life in general, is what can I learn from this (or what is good about this)? In life there are always going to be adverse events. Part of our resiliency is not just surviving them but learning from them and moving on. It's very easy to just say, "Oh, I'm not good enough," or "That person betrayed me," instead of asking, "What is good about this?" and learning something. I've seen novice traders get angry at the market, and that anger threatens their portfolio more than it helps. Asking questions such as, "What can I learn from this?" empowers us to control our lives rather than remain victims of our circumstances.

CONCLUSION

We all have a number that controls our lives, whether it be the number of years we expect to live or an income figure we subconsciously gravitate toward. In investing, this number is our goal for the value of our account and when our account reaches that value, we self-sabotage and crash the account, or we subconsciously create crises in our lives. A typical example would be that of someone who's saving for college but the dishwasher keeps breaking, or the car repeatedly needs work, so the long-term goal of creating a college fund is never reached. Lottery winners tend to spend everything they're awarded and then more. If they were in debt before winning the lottery, they tend to be even more in debt within a few years after their lottery wins. So wealth is as much a state of mind as it is a balance in our investment account. Our subconscious forces dictate how much we think we're worth.

As a young intern, my number was in the minus column. But I knew that wasn't where I wanted it to be. So I learned to develop investing systems that are simple, yet robust, and that have helped me semi-retire at the age of 45. Investing doesn't have to be complicated or intimidating or time consuming; it just requires a little discipline. But before I could be successful with even these simple systems, I had to find and deal with my own self-sabotaging roadblocks.

Most physicians are clueless about investing systems and invest without a systematic approach. I know colleagues who don't even open their investment statements. Why not? My guesses are that they are afraid of money in general or that it's a hassle for them. Maybe they don't want to open up and see how little they have. But I believe the number-one reason they don't open their statements is that they don't understand those statements or what's going on in their portfolio. Doctors are trained to have answers, so if they look at statements they don't understand, they avoid them. Not understanding makes them uncomfortable; it's not part of their identity. A smoker who is quitting will count the days since he had his last cigarette and, eventually, cave in to desire; a smoker who has successfully quit, if offered a cigarette, easily refuses with "Sorry, I'm not a smoker." An identity change is everything. Someone who can read an X-ray will read them all day. These physicians will feel good about the work they have done. But if you don't understand something as basic as reading a brokerage statement and seeing where your money is, chances are you'll avoid it. I've known colleagues who, despite having money managers, suffered great losses during the last two bear markets of the twenty-first century. They need not have experienced such losses had their managers used a slightly more sophisticated system than just dollar cost averaging their accounts in a pie chart with rebalancing. I believe that systematic investing helps us become better investors.

I've presented four systems in this book that have helped me and that require minimum effort per month. Personal finance is an important part of our lives. To master the impact and importance of money in our lives—both emotionally and mechanically—is to grow in a way that enriches us more than just financially.

In the past 19 years, I've gone from a mountain of credit card debt and no knowledge about money to financial literacy and the ability to semi-retire. I lead a life that contributes more than I could otherwise have contributed to my family, loved ones, and community, and now I'm able to reach out to an expanded community through this book.

I don't know if there's any one secret to success, but a key component would be the ability to recognize an opportunity of a lifetime and take advantage of it during the lifetime of the opportunity. This means action is crucial but only action that is tempered with feedback from emotional experiences. We must recognize that emotions play an extremely important, if unstated, role in our lives. Emotions underlie whether we end up abundant or destitute or live lives of quiet desperation. Being able to control or, at least, identify our emotions not only boosts our success in personal finance but also in other parts of our lives, such as our relationships, our health, and our careers.

It is true that some good traders say they follow their guts. But if you question these traders, they'll admit they've learned through many mistakes of their own in order to attain this level of intuition. One way we can shortcut this learning curve is to use systems to build on our intuitions before our emotions get the best of us. Through experience, we eventually perform on a more subconscious level and thus become more efficient. In time, our gut definitely does become more reliable, but before we are able to reach this level of unconscious competency, we must admit our initial level of unconscious incompetency.

All learning, including financial learning, progresses through four stages: unconscious incompetency (we think we can invest and cannot understand why we are not successful), conscious incompetency (we are consciously, and perhaps, painfully aware of our own ignorance and incompetence in the market), conscious competency (being able to mechanically implement successful strategies), and unconscious competency (the gut feeling of successful traders, based on years of successful investing).

I have outlined four simple investment systems in this book. But they only work if you actually implement them. It is very important to learn how to rely on a system before you begin to invest in the market, recognizing that once you have money in the market, your emotions become such an overwhelming force in your decision making that they can lead you to veer off-course, follow the herd, and destroy your account.

We started out with dollar cost averaging. Technically, it's not a system by itself because there is no exit strategy. But it is a simple one-rule structure that can be applied to almost anything else, such as dollar cost averaging into a stock, dollar cost averaging into a mutual fund, or dollar cost averaging into another system. A money manager would have you dollar cost averaging into either a pie chart or some other model, such as a bond ladder system. The strength of dollar cost averaging is that, if done correctly, it can lower the average cost of entry, and thus increase the likelihood of returning a profit. Its weakness is that dollar cost averaging can also crash your account if the underlying stock or mutual fund or system also crashes. Because dollar cost averaging has no exit strategy, if you rely on this particular system for retirement, you can only hope that the market is relatively high by the time you retire and not on a downward trend when you stop contributing and start withdrawing.

The 20-month moving average is a way to detect when it is fairly safe to be in stocks (in this book we have used the example of the S&P 500 index), and when it is dangerous to be in stocks. By switching between stocks and bonds, during reasonably safe and comparatively dangerous times of the market, we can increase our overall cumulative return by cutting out large portions of the bear markets and diversifying over time, rather than diversifying statically by means of a pie chart. We do not seek to eliminate all losses, merely the larger, longer-term losses. Because there is a definite exit strategy with the 20-month moving average, we are not left to rely solely on hope. Its weakness is that markets will always have relatively small downturns in addition to the big bear markets, and occasionally, these small downturns can be large enough to cause a whipsaw, but these small downturns are somewhat minor compared to what could happen if we had just held through a large bear market.

The MRI is a system that protects us by utilizing both an index fund and an inverse index fund. In this way, theoretically, something is always going up. It works by automatically rotating our portfolio into a stronger trend. This is the MRI autocorrecting mechanism. Its strength is that it both mitigates bear markets and produces increased returns. A weakness of the MRI system is that it is more complex, so monthly monitoring is mandatory. Another weakness of the system is that we're always rotating into the dominant trend, but sometimes the trend is not clear, thus MRI can be prone to whipsaws, dragging down overall performance.

Then, we come to the fourth system of investing, the system that deals with stock tips. Individual stocks are particularly risky in that stocks have idiosyncratic risk; stock-specific news can tank the stock overnight.

If you do come across a stock tip you strongly believe in, go ahead and use 4 percent of your account to play it, but remember to control your risk by using some type of stop loss that ratchets up as the stock rises. The 25 percent trailing-stop-loss system is for those times when we hear of a "sure thing," or potentially great investment, and our human psychological need to not miss out on this opportunity kicks in. If we approach these opportunities in a systematic fashion, such as adequate position sizing and utilizing a 25 percent trailing stop loss, we can invest in them, and if we're wrong, we won't lose that much money. However, if we are right, we will reap the fruits of our actions and still retain bragging rights. It's the best of both worlds. The downside to this system is that there is still the potential for loss, albeit small. Stocks, more likely than mutual funds, can gap down and, sometimes, gap down very far below your stop loss, and you may suffer losses greater than you anticipated. Investing this way is also relatively boring, compared to the casino-like story that got us interested in the stock to begin with. And when you have a small amount, and the stock goes up, you're not as excited as those who invested their whole account. But if the stock keeps going up, you will, eventually, use more and more of your account to buy more and more stock. If the stock goes down, and most of them do, at least you live to trade another day.

When I explain my investing strategies to my colleagues and other physicians, they appear amazed that not only do these investment systems exist but also that these systems are simple enough for even a busy professional to implement effectively. Many of these physicians, for the first time, have hope for the future. However, instead of employing these investing systems themselves, they often ask me if I would invest for them. With the Wealthy Doctor Institute, I can. However, I would much rather empower my community to take control of their own finances than be reliant on money managers using systems that they don't understand.

On the Wealthy Doctor Institute website I update information regularly through blogs and monthly video updates. This book describes the methods I use. However, many investors want updates to follow along, either to make sure their own calculations are correct or to ask questions. Updates are like training wheels; they help new investors to get used to a system. My purpose for the Wealthy Doctor Institute is to provide additional information and services to help doctors become better investors.

Just as you wish you'd started investing 20 years ago, 20 years from now, you'll wish you had started today. Reading this book is a good beginning, but it's not enough. You need to take action now. If you stop now, momentum stops, and you'll have to go through the whole process of becoming emotionally ready again to take action in the future. Don't allow your fears to stop you from investing intelligently or from looking into other ways to develop your investing competence. Fears serve a purpose: they send the message that you should prepare. No matter what moves you make in investing, there will always be a weak spot. Learn your weak spots and the emotions behind them. Fears can be competently dealt with, through preparation and habituation. The fears you experienced as a medical student when you saw your first patient or ran your first code as an intern are familiar old friends of yours now. We grow stronger by stepping away from our comfort zone. You've taken the first step by reading this book and now have one more tool with which to face future challenges.

AUTHOR'S BIO

David Yeh, MD, is a practicing physician, speaker, author, and investment advisor.

David graduated from Cornell University and New York University School of Medicine. He is board certified in radiology and nuclear medicine. He is also a Registered Investment Advisor and a member of Mensa.

David combines the tools of traditional money managers, the risk mitigation techniques of active market traders, and the skills of a diagnostic physician, including pattern recognition and quantitative analysis, to develop novel investment systems tailored for busy doctors. In less than 20 years of beginning his professional career, he has semi-retired at the age of 45.

He lives in Naperville, Illinois, with his wife and son.

BOOK DISCLOSURE STATEMENT

This book is not intended to offer personalized financial advice for any specific situation. Each individual's financial situation is unique, and any information in this presentation cannot be relied upon or considered personalized financial advice. References to specific securities are not intended to address readers' particular financial situations. Past performance is not indicative of future performance. None of the information presented in this book is reflective of any actual accounts. Forecasting a status or trend is not a guarantee of direction or performance. Charts and graphs in and of themselves cannot predict price movements. The charts used in this presentation should not be considered a solicitation for the purchase or sale of any individual security shown. All investing involves risk, and appropriate financial advice should be sought for a particular situation before the implementation of any strategy discussed herein. Returns may not be reflective of all applicable fees and expenses.

BACK-TESTED PERFORMANCE DISCLOSURE STATEMENT

B ack-tested performance is *not* an indicator of actual future results. There are limitations inherent in hypothetical results. In particular, the performance results do not represent the results of actual trading using client assets but were achieved by means of the retroactive application of a back-tested model that was designed with the benefit of hindsight. The results reflect the performance of a strategy not historically offered to investors and do *not* represent returns that any investor actually attained. Back-tested results are calculated by the retroactive application of a model constructed on the basis of historical data and based on assumptions integral to the model that may or may not be testable and are subject to losses.

Back-tested performance has inherent limitations. Specifically, back-tested results do not reflect actual trading, the effect of material economic and market factors on the decision-making process, or the skill of the adviser. Since trades have not actually been executed, results may have undercompensated or overcompensated for the impact, if any, of certain market factors, such as lack of liquidity, and may not reflect the impact that certain economic or market factors may have had on the decision-making process. Further, back-testing allows the security selection methodology to be adjusted until past returns are maximized. Actual performance may differ significantly from back-tested performance.

Printed in the USA
CPSIA information can be obtained
at www.ICGtesting.com
JSHW011949290424
62140JS00019B/723

9 781599 325521